THE ULTIMATE B2B MARKETING LIST:

200+ INNOVATIVE TACTICS YOU NEED TO TRY

DON'T ASK WHAT EVERYBODY IS DOING, INSTEAD ASK: WHAT IS NOBODY DOING?

BONUS INSIDE:
AN ESSENTIAL GUIDE TO CHATGPT

JESSICA SCHWARZE

DISCLAIMER

The information contained in this book is intended for general informational purposes only. The tactics and strategies described may not be suitable for every business and should be customised to fit the unique needs and goals of each individual business. It is important to conduct your own research and due diligence before implementing any of the ideas presented in this book. The author and publisher of this book cannot be held liable for any actions taken based on the information provided. As always, it is recommended to seek the advice of a professional before making any business decisions.

This book was completed with the help of ChatGPT, a language model trained by OpenAI, especially for editing purposes.

Copyright © 2023 Jessica Schwarze

All Rights Reserved. This book, or parts thereof, may not be reproduced in any form or by any means, electronic or mechanical, including photocopying, recording or any information storage or retrieval system now known or to be invented, without the written permission of the author.

I dedicate this book to

Singgih Wandojo,

your guidance as my manager during my time at **SAP** was invaluable.

You set the foundation for my success in B2B Marketing, and I am forever grateful for your unwavering belief in me. Thank you for being an inspiration and mentor in my early years in B2B software marketing.

and

Graham McColough,

I am incredibly appreciative for the opportunity you gave me to join **Software AG** and take on my first APAC regional role. Your bringing me to the company was a turning point in my professional journey. Thank you for making my dream of working in a regional role at a global company a reality.

with gratitude,

Jessica

"Too often we convince ourselves that massive results require massive action."

James Clear
Author of New York Times Bestseller
"Atomic Habits"[1]

---

[1] Clear, J. (2018). Atomic Habits: An Easy & Proven Way to Build Good Habits & Break Bad Ones. Penguin.

TABLE OF CONTENTS

Introduction 1
    My Letter To You... 2
    Why Listen To Me?.. 4
    What Is B2b Marketing? 5
    The Four Must-Know Trends In B2B Marketing........................ 6

The ChatGPT Essential Guide: A B2B Marketer's Guide To Unleashing The Full Potential Of AI 11
    Why ChatGPT Is A Game-Changer For Marketers 12
    Uses Of ChatGPT In B2B Marketing.. 13
    Getting Started With ChatGPT.. 17
    ChatGPT Syntax And Commands... 18
    "Promptology"... 19
    Limitations Of ChatGPT 24
    ChatGPT Strategies 26
    The Future Of ChatGPT In Marketing 28
    Examples Of ChatGPT Prompts & Answers............................. 29

Part One: Getting To Know Your Dream Buyers....................... 37
    Introduction 38
    Three Steps To Identify And Build Your ICP........................... 39
    Innovative Tactics To Refine Your ICP 41

Tools To Help You In Your Buyer Research 46

Part Two: Crafting Killer Content 48

    Introduction 49

    Five Steps To Improve The Effectiveness Of Your Content Strategy 51

    Innovative Tactics For Content Development 53

    Ad Content Building Tactics 63

    Content Building Techniques 68

    Improve Your Existing Content 73

    Tools For Content Development 79

Part Three: Making A Visual Impact 82

    Visuals 83

    Videos 90

Part Four: Climbing The Search Engine Rankings 101

    Search Engine Optimisation 102

    Search Engine Marketing 123

Part Five: Unleashing The Power Of Social Media 132

    Introduction 133

    Innovative Tactics To Succeed In Social Media 136

    The Four Key B2B Social Media Platforms 140

Part Six: Exploring Other Innovative Tactics 171

    Introduction 172

    Physical Events 173

Website 179

Others: 182

Part Seven: Mastering Conversion Optimisation 188

Introduction 189

Tactics To Improve Conversion Rates Across The Funnel 191

Tools For Conversion Optimisation 208

Part Eight: Aligning Sales & Marketing: A Match Made In Heaven ... 212

Introduction 213

Tactics For Sales & Marketing Alignment 215

Tools For Sales And Marketing Alignment 220

Part Nine: Keeping Customers Coming Back For More 221

Introduction 222

Tactics For Customer Retention 223

Tools For Customer Retention 227

Closing Remarks 229

Glossary 230

INTRODUCTION

MY LETTER TO YOU

Dear Reader,

I am delighted you bought this book! As you are about to learn, this book is packed with practical marketing tactics that are both innovative and cost-effective (many of them are free!).

While it is certainly important to have a solid marketing strategy in place, it is also important to recognize that many tactics outlined in this book can be implemented right away and benefit organisations regardless of whether their strategies have been fully developed. These tactics are "strategy-agnostic" and can be useful for any company no matter their overall marketing approach.

I urge you to always work with marketing tactics in a systematic and methodical way. Align them with your marketing goals and target audience and integrate them into your overall marketing efforts. Then success is on its way!

Thank you for giving me the opportunity to share my insights with you, to inspire, motivate, and contribute to your success.

Sincerely,

Jessica Schwarze

P.S. Please note that in this book, I am using the term "tactics" in a broad sense to encompass a range of tools, tips, and tricks.

Marketing tactics should not be confused with marketing strategy. A marketing strategy is a long-term plan that outlines the steps needed to achieve a specific goal, while tactics are the specific actions taken to carry out the planned strategy. In other words, tactics represent the execution or action phase of a marketing plan.

P.P.S. I really wish I had more visuals in this edition. Unfortunately, time constraints did not allow for their inclusion. The next editions will be filled with images, charts, and screenshots to enhance your reading experience.

WHY LISTEN TO ME?

I have been in B2B (Business to Business) Marketing for more than 25 years. I feel humbled to have dedicated a quarter of a century to this field, and the realisation brings a big smile to my face!

Over the years, I have amassed a wealth of marketing knowledge and experience, and I am eager to share them with you. Throughout my career, I have won awards for my innovative ideas that have made a real impact.

I have worked with a wide range of companies, from large multinational organisations to small start-ups. Throughout my career I have had the privilege of working with some of the best minds in B2B from around the world.

I have managed diverse teams and big to small budgets and have participated in numerous marketing enablement programs both internally and externally.

I continue to read countless books and material on marketing and related topics. And so, I hope I can provide you with a well-rounded perspective on innovative B2B marketing tactics.

Although my background is focused in the complex tech industry, I am confident that professionals in other industries can also gain value from this book.

Furthermore, any professional in B2B marketing, as well as general marketers, will be able to find tactics and ideas that can be implemented in their own work.

I truly hope you feel the same way.

WHAT IS B2B MARKETING?

Business to Business (B2B) marketing is all about promoting products or services to other businesses and organisations. It's different from Business to Consumer (B2C) marketing (which targets consumers) in that B2B is more informational and straightforward. That's because business purchase decisions are often based on the bottom-line revenue impact and return on investment (ROI).

In today's business world, B2B marketers often must sell to buying committees with multiple stakeholders, which can be a bit tricky. But with access to more accurate data, it's becoming easier for B2B marketers to personalise their approach and reach buyers with relevant information.

Any company that sells to other companies can benefit from B2B marketing. B2B can include businesses in IT and Technology, manufacturing, consulting and professional services, wholesale and distribution, transportation, and logistics and many more.

When it comes to creating a B2B marketing strategy, it's important to have a clear vision and specific, measurable goals. You'll also want to define your market and buyer persona, identify the best tactics and channels for reaching your target audience, and create assets and campaigns that align with your goals. Finally, it's crucial to measure and improve your strategy on an ongoing basis.

THE FOUR MUST-KNOW TRENDS IN B2B MARKETING

There are many important trends in B2B marketing, but I have chosen to focus on these four key trends in building my list of marketing tactics, as outlined below.

Self-Service Buying

In B2B, 57% - 70% of the buying decisions are made BEFORE buyers even talk to a company and their sales team.[2] Buyers are increasingly doing their own research and handling more of the purchasing process themselves before reaching out to their potential vendors.

In fact, TrustRadius' 2022 B2B Buying Disconnect report[3] found that almost all buyers prefer to self-serve part or all of the buying journey, an increase of 13% from the previous year. As a result, B2B companies must provide purpose-built websites and new digital channels that drive sales performance.

While sales teams have traditionally played a central role in this process, marketing teams are now leading the way in creating digitally rich experiences that support self-learning and help customers navigate the complexities of choosing products and services.

Companies with strong marketing teams that:
- are fully aligned with the sales organisation and
- prioritise a digital-first approach

are likely to see more successful sales outcomes compared to those that

---

[2] https://www.wbresearch.com/relationship-between-b2b-buying-content-sales-changed-insights
[3] https://www.trustradius.com/vendor-blog/2022-b2b-buying-disconnect-the-age-of-the-self-serve-buyer

are slow to adapt.

You will see that most tactics in this book are focused on digital marketing, and the optimisation of a company's digital presence.

Marketing Efficiency

After going through the various challenges brought on by the Covid-19 pandemic, the collective business mindset was centred on growth. Companies were eager to make up for lost time and revenue and were focused on expanding their operations and increasing their market share.

However, as the year progressed, and inflation hit, things changed once again. Suddenly, it was no longer just about growing at all costs; it was about efficient growth. Companies had to find ways to achieve growth while minimising costs and marketers are being forced to do more with less.

The focus on efficient growth means that organisations will need to be smart about how they allocate their resources and prioritise the most promising accounts and opportunities. This may involve reviewing their entire go-to-market strategy and doubling down on the most cost-efficient areas. Companies will need to lean on automation to streamline processes, reduce errors, and free up human resources to focus on more value-adding tasks.

I believe that my book can be an invaluable resource for marketers who are looking to do more with less.

The list of tactics is practical and actionable and will help marketers identify ideas that can enhance campaign results, drive pipeline, and achieve other business objectives.

Authenticity

Recently, an important (and positive!) trend in content is gaining prominence: namely, the customers' desire for authenticity and honesty.

Businesses today are seeking out genuine, unedited content rather than perfection. This trend has been growing in recent years and is expected to continue.

This shift away from polished, staged content means that it is no longer necessary for B2B businesses to strive for perfect video production, appearance, or only sharing positive messages.

In fact, the more real and raw the content, the more effective it is likely to be. This allows for a more authentic representation of the company, its products or services, and its values, which can help to build trust and credibility with potential clients.

However, authenticity in marketing is a growing challenge because it is becoming more difficult for brands to maintain a consistent and genuine image in the digital world. This is due to the proliferation of channels and campaigns, as well as the increasing savvy generation of buyers who are more likely to recognize insincerity.

To be authentic, companies must be intentional and mindful in their marketing efforts and ensure that their brand reflects the shared passion and mission of the team. Authentic marketing also involves making customers feel like they are part of the brand's community.

In this book, I am sharing several ideas to help you drive authenticity for your organisation.

ChatGPT

A week after the release of ChatGPT, I published a blog "I tried ChatGPT and WOW" [4].

The use of artificial intelligence (AI) capabilities by companies has increased significantly in recent years, according to a review by McKinsey. As a result, there is growing interest in how ChatGPT, a tool with generative AI capabilities, can be used by businesses. It is important for professionals in the field of marketing and data to be aware of ChatGPT's capabilities and limitations to build a successful career.

In marketing, ChatGPT is revolutionising the way content is created, and will disrupt how the content is distributed and consumed. ChatGPT will not only help content creators make stronger content, but it drastically reduces the time needed to do so. With ChatGPT, EVERYONE can be an excellent content creator. There are of course some limitations, because ChatGPT is in its infancy stage or an early research release, and

---

[4] https://www.linkedin.com/pulse/marketer-i-tried-chatgpt-wow-jessica-schwarze/

there is much anticipation regarding the imminent release of ChatGPT-4.

It is very hard to overestimate how ChatGPT will change the face of B2B Marketing.

Below is the text written by ChatGPT on how it will impact B2B Marketing:

> *"ChatGPT, also known as Chat Generative Pre-training Transformer, is a state-of-the-art language model developed by OpenAI that can generate human-like text in real-time. In the world of B2B marketing, ChatGPT is revolutionising the way companies engage with their target audience by providing personalised and intelligent responses to customer inquiries and interactions.*
>
> *Another way ChatGPT is revolutionising B2B marketing is by providing personalised and targeted content to customers. By analysing customer data and interactions, ChatGPT can generate customised marketing messages and content that align with the customer's interests and needs. This helps companies build stronger relationships with their target audience and increase the chances of making a sale.*
>
> *Overall, ChatGPT and similar AI technologies can be powerful tools for B2B marketers, helping to automate and optimise various aspects of marketing campaigns and customer interactions."*

As pointed out by ChatGPT, there are similar AI Technologies out there and we can see that ChatGPT has significantly contributed to the growth, demand, and awareness of artificial intelligence in general.

"AI will not replace humans, but humans who do not embrace AI will be replaced by humans who do".

Anonymous

> **TIP:** A new platform has been developed recently to help identify the right AI for what we are planning to do. It is called <u>thereisanaiforthat</u> which lists 700+ AI technologies and is updated daily. You can search by use case.

Turn the page and let's get started with the ChatGPT Guide.

THE CHATGPT ESSENTIAL GUIDE: A B2B MARKETER'S GUIDE TO UNLEASHING THE FULL POTENTIAL OF AI

WHY CHATGPT IS A GAME-CHANGER FOR MARKETERS

ChatGPT represents a major shift in the way that B2B marketers can reach and engage with their audiences. Here are a few key reasons why ChatGPT is a game-changer for marketers (courtesy ChatGPT!):

1. **Enhanced efficiency and scalability:** ChatGPT allow marketers to automate and streamline many of the tasks that are traditionally time-consuming and resource-intensive, such as creating personalised content or conducting market research. This can free up valuable time and resources that can be better spent on other areas of the business

2. **Greater flexibility and adaptability:** With ChatGPT, marketers can quickly and easily generate a wide range of content and messaging, making it easier to test and optimise their marketing efforts in real-time. This allows marketers to be more agile and responsive to changing market conditions and customer needs.

3. **Improved customer experiences:** By leveraging ChatGPT to create personalised, relevant content and communications, marketers can deliver more meaningful and engaging experiences for their customers. This can lead to increased customer loyalty and lifetime value.

4. **Enhanced creativity and innovation:** ChatGPT can provide marketers with new and unconventional ideas and insights that can help them think outside the box and come up with fresh, innovative marketing approaches.

USES OF CHATGPT IN B2B MARKETING

Here is a list of uses for ChatGPT based on my experience so far (the list is by no means exhaustive!)

Research and Brainstorming:
- Keywords (hopefully soon with search volume data)
- Keyword synonyms
- Topics related to a keyword
- Keyword classification or clustering (e.g., based on search intent, semantic relevance etc)
- Long Form Keyword
- Competitor Information
- Job titles related to a field
- Countries in a region
- Marketing plan/calendar
- Content plan/calendar
- Content distribution channels
- Blog/article or content ideas
- Hashtags
- Marketing plan/calendar
- Content plan/calendar
- Content distribution channels
- Popular Blogs in a specific topic for link building

Personalization and targeting:
- Personalised email campaigns
- Personalised social media content
- Personalised chatbot interactions
- Targeted lead-generation content

Customer research and insight generation:
- Generating customer profile
- Analysing customer feedback
- Generating customer personas
- Conducting market research
- Generating customer insight

Content generation:
- Blog posts
- Articles
- Product descriptions
- Customer testimonials
- Customer reviews
- Landing pages
- Whitepapers
- eBooks
- Infographics
- Slides
- Videos
- Short videos
- Proposals
- Quizzes
- Emails

- Social media posts
- Tweets
- Hooks for social media
- Comments
- Newsletter content
- Headlines
- Press releases
- Draft testimonials/review ideas for customers
- Customer quotes for social media banners
- Ad copies/offers
- Lead-generation content (such as landing pages, whitepapers, and eBooks)
- FAQs
- Podcast scripts
- Master of ceremony scripts
- Scripts for slides
- Scripts for videos and short videos
- Personalised email content (including subject lines, body copy, and calls to action)
- Social media content (such as posts, tweets, and comments)
- Newsletter welcome messages

Editing copies:
- Paraphrasing
- Spell Checking
- Checking for plagiarism
- Summarising
- Converting into bullet points

- Changing style
- Adding humour
- Translating
- Repurposing Content into different formats
- Word Count: Lengthening or shortening your text

Building:
- Marketing plans
- Product launch plans
- Social media calendars
- Social media strategies
- Content calendars
- Buyer persona/avatars
- AdWords plans
- A Brand Guidelines

GETTING STARTED WITH CHATGPT

It is very simple to start with ChatGPT!

To use ChatGPT, you'll need to create an account on the ChatGPT website or download the app from the App Store or Google Play.

This will typically require you to provide some basic information such as your name and email address, to set the password and to agree to the terms of service.

Start using ChatGPT by running ChatGPT commands from the command line.

Note: In this guide, I am not covering the command-line interface/API or obtaining the API key for ChatGPT due to a lack of my personal experience and the technical nature of the topic. I do not want to provide inaccurate information to readers and therefore I have chosen not to include the command-line interface here.

CHATGPT SYNTAX AND COMMANDS

As a marketer, understanding the basics of ChatGPT syntax and commands is critical to leverage the full power of this powerful AI tool. Here are a few key concepts:

1. **Syntax**: ChatGPT uses a specific syntax, or set of rules, for formatting and organising its commands. This syntax is based on the Python programming language and involves using specific keywords, punctuation, and structures to create valid commands.

2. **Commands:** ChatGPT supports a range of commands that allow you to perform various marketing-related tasks, such as generating personalised content, conducting market research, or managing your ChatGPT environment. Some common ChatGPT commands for marketing include prompt, custom, and train. (Pay attention to prompt commands or prompts, which I will elaborate further).

3. **Arguments:** Many ChatGPT commands accept one or more arguments, which are additional pieces of information that are used to specify the details of the command. For example, the prompt command typically accepts a string argument that specifies the text prompt to be used, while the custom command accepts arguments that specify the custom prompt and response pairs to be added to the model.

4. **Options:** Some ChatGPT commands also support options, which are additional parameters that can be used to modify the behaviour of the command. Options are typically specified using the -- syntax, followed by the option name and a value. For example, the prompt command supports the --max-tokens option, which specifies the maximum number of tokens (i.e., words) to generate in response to the prompt.

"PROMPTOLOGY"

The Science of Creating Effective Prompts for AI

Now let's delve deeper into prompts for ChatGPT, as it is key in getting the most out of it. Prompts has become such a focus that some suggest a new science will emerge, coined "Promptology" or the science of creating effective prompts for AI. Mastering prompts is key in getting the best results from ChatGPT.

Here are some strategies to inspire you:

1. Tell ChatGPT about the writing style you want

You can emulate the style of your favourite personalities or people who inspire you. They can be writers or thought leaders in your field.

You can also indicate the style you are after, for example the various business writing styles:

instructional/educational (for user manuals, or how to content, for example) informational (whitepapers, reports), persuasive (email drip copies), and transactional (day to day official communications, official letters); simple to understand, conversational, scientific, legal, formal, informal and even humorous.

Examples:

- *"Give me 10 high converting headlines using the principles of Breakthrough Advertising by Eugene Schwartz, that are less than 250 characters."*

- *"Give me 10 title options for my blog on the top 3 marketing trends in 2023 in the style of Gary Vaynerchuk"*

2. Add parameters in your request

The length/ word count / character count

The number of options it provides you

3. Ask for SEO Optimised Content

Example: "Give me SEO optimised sub-headlines for my blog entitled…"

4. Ask ChatGPT to provide the source of facts, statistics and trends related to a topic and to support your claims in your content.

Example: "Provide me supporting data with sources to my claim that authenticity is gaining importance in B2B Marketing"

Awesome ChatGPT Prompts by GitHub

GitHub has released a list "Awesome ChatGPT Prompts"

Below I selected a few that were particularly useful for me:

Act as a Plagiarism Checker

I want you to act as an English translator, spelling corrector and improver. I will speak to you in any language, and you will detect the language, translate it and answer in the corrected and improved version of my text, in English. I want you to replace my simplified A0-level words and sentences with more beautiful and elegant, upper-level English words and sentences. Keep the meaning the same but make them more literary. I want you to only reply to the correction, the improvements and nothing else, do not write explanations.

Act as a Storyteller

I want you to act as a storyteller. You will come up with entertaining stories that are engaging, imaginative and captivating for the audience. It can be fairy tales, educational stories or any other type of stories which has the potential to capture people's attention and imagination. Depending on the target audience, you may choose specific themes or topics for your storytelling session e.g., if it's children then you can talk about animals, If it's adults then history-based tales might engage them better etc. My first request is "I need an interesting story on perseverance."

Act as a Motivational Speaker

I want you to act as a motivational speaker. Put together words that inspire action and make people feel empowered to do something beyond their abilities. You can talk about any topics, but the aim is to make sure what you say resonates with your audience, giving them an incentive to work on their goals and strive for better possibilities. My first request is "I need a speech about how everyone should never give up."

Act as a fancy Title Generator

I want you to act as a fancy title generator. I will type keywords via comma, and you will reply with fancy titles. My first keywords are: API, test, automation.

Act as a Statistician

I want to act as a Statistician. I will provide you with details related to statistics. You should have knowledge of statistics terminology, statistical distributions, confidence interval, probability, hypothesis testing and statistical charts. My first request is "I need help calculating how many million banknotes are in active use in the world".

ChatGPT can also help you with recommending effective prompts!

Act as a Prompt Generator

I want you to act as a prompt generator. Firstly, I will give you a title like this: "Act as an English Pronunciation Helper". Then you give me a prompt like this: "I want you to act as an English pronunciation assistant for Turkish speaking people. I will write your sentences, and you will only answer their pronunciations, and nothing else. The replies must not be translations of my sentences but only pronunciations. Pronunciations should use Turkish Latin letters for phonetics. Do not write explanations on replies. My first sentence is "how is the weather in Istanbul?" You should adapt the sample prompt according to the title I gave. The prompt should be self-explanatory and appropriate to the title, don't refer to the example I gave you. My first title is "Act as a Code Review Helper" (Give me prompt only)

From which I generated the prompt as a Marketing expert:

Act as a Marketing Expert

"I want you to act as a marketing expert and provide guidance on how to effectively promote a new product to a target audience. Your responses should focus on providing specific strategies and tactics for creating and executing a successful marketing campaign. Please do not provide general information about marketing or general business advice. Instead, focus on providing practical, actionable steps for promoting a specific product. As an example, you can consider a scenario where the product is a new organic skincare line targeting millennial women. How would you go about promoting this product to this audience?"

Follow Up Prompts:

Once ChatGPT provides a response, you can always "regenerate a response" or prompt ChatGPT further with these phrases:

- Give me more options
- Give me more examples
- Longer. Shorter.
- More in-depth
- In a more inviting tone. More formal. Less Formal. In a friendlier tone. Even friendlier.
- In table format
- Expand on that
- In First Person/ Third person

- Translate to (language)

LIMITATIONS OF CHATGPT

While ChatGPT is a fantastic tool, it's not without its limitations. Here are six of them:

1. The output is only as good as the input. Keep in mind that ChatGPT's output is only as good as the input it receives. If you're not clear about what you're asking or don't have a solid understanding of the subject matter, the answers ChatGPT provides may be too general and may not be useful. It's crucial to have a strong grasp of both the input you give ChatGPT and the topic you're asking about.

2. Data may be outdated or inaccurate. One limitation of ChatGPT is that the data it is trained on may be outdated or inaccurate. ChatGPT is a large language model that has been trained on a vast amount of data from the internet, including texts, articles, and websites. While this data can provide a wealth of knowledge and information, it is important to note that it may not always be up-to-date or completely accurate. For example, ChatGPT may provide outdated information about current events, technology, or scientific discoveries, as it is not able to access new information once it has been trained.

1. Additionally, the data that ChatGPT is trained on may contain inaccuracies or errors, which could lead to the model providing incorrect or misleading answers to questions. It is important to keep this limitation in mind when using ChatGPT and to verify the accuracy and timeliness of the information it provides. It is also a good idea to use other sources of information to cross-reference and confirm the accuracy of ChatGPT's responses.

2. The output is often broad and general, repetitive, and redundant. Another limitation of ChatGPT is that its output can often be broad, general, repetitive, and redundant. For example, it frequently uses the word 'overall' in its conclusions and describes various platforms as 'a valuable tool.' In some cases, it may even describe two different tools that offer similar services in the same way, word for word.

3. The content generated by ChatGPT does not necessarily follow your

brand voice and messaging. You can include the preferred brand style in your prompt, but it is critical for businesses to review and edit the content generated by Chat GPT to ensure it is aligned with your brand voice and messaging always carefully.

4. It cannot replicate human judgement, emotional intelligence, and experience. ChatGPT is very good at aggregating information from different sources and providing generic recommendations, but it can't replicate judgement, emotional intelligence, and experience. It can't make decisions or provide recommendations based on real-world experience or expertise. Therefore, it's important to use ChatGPT as a tool to supplement your own knowledge and expertise, rather than relying on it to make important decisions or provide specific recommendations.

5. AI Detectors will impact your content ranking. Soon, AI generated content may not rank high in Google or other search engines. It is very likely that Google and other search engines update their algorithms to detect whether articles or other types of content have been written by AI and not rank them highly in search results. There are already tools available that can identify AI-generated content, and these tools will only become more sophisticated over time.An update that Google has recently made is adding a new "E" to their E-A-T algorithm.Google E-A-T algorithm stands for expertise, authority, and trust. Recently, Google decided to add an extra "E" to E-A-T, making it E-E-A-T and this new "E" stands for experience.While expertise and experience may seem similar, they are distinct in that expertise refers to knowledge and skills in a particular field, while experience refers to personal or hands-on involvement in a particular topic. Experience is something that is difficult to replicate using AI, at least for now.

CHATGPT STRATEGIES

Considering the above limitations, below are the strategies to address them:

1. Study "Promptology" and continuously experiment with different prompts to see what works best for your audience.
2. Always use prompts and responses that reflect your subject matter, e.g., your marketing goals. In this case, if you are looking to generate lead-generation content, you might use prompts that focus on pain points and solutions, and responses that highlight the benefits of your products or services.
3. Always refine any content generated by ChatGPT and add your own spin to ensure that it's uniquely your own. I have found that the copy is often repetitive. Some definitions of new marketing concepts can be downright wrong. Therefore, it is important for you as the subject matter expert to review and approve.
4. To ensure that the content generated by ChatGPT aligns with your brand's voice and messaging, it's important to review and edit them carefully and regularly. Never neglect to maintain your branding and style guidelines. When using ChatGPT for marketing content, make sure to keep your brand's tone, voice, and style in mind and carefully review and edit the output to ensure it stays consistent with your brand's identity and messaging.
5. Continually test and optimise your ChatGPT settings to see what works best for you and your audience. Don't be afraid to think outside the box and seek out new and creative ways to use ChatGPT for marketing. There are many ways that have yet to be explored, so stay open to new ideas and approaches.
6. Do not over rely on ChatGPT. While ChatGPT is a powerful tool, it is important to remember that it is just one part of your marketing strategy. Look for opportunities to leverage its power in conjunction with other marketing efforts. Consider ChatGPT as just one tool in

your entire marketing toolkit, and that it can be more effective when used in combination with other tools and tactics.

7. Use extensions, to supercharge your ChatGPT:

Great Extensions for ChatGPT

WebChatGPT to augment your ChatGPT prompts with relevant results from the web because ChatGPT cannot scrape the web and has limited data of the world after 2021.

ChatGPT for Search Engines extension, to view ChatGPT results on Google or Bing!

The Merlin extension to use ChatGPT on *any* website (search engines, Gmail, Google Sheets, or just anywhere).

ChatGPT Prompt Genius (formerly History) to save your prompts in PNG, PDF, Markdown and more!

TweetGPT writes tweets with ChatGPT

ChatGPT Writer generates entire emails and messages based on a few keywords that you input using ChatGPT AI. All sites are supported.

YouTube Summary with ChatGPT to generate text transcripts of any Youtube Videos.

ShareGPT to share your ChatGPT prompts with the world with one click.

VoiceCommand ChatGPT Use voice commands for your ChatGPT

ChatGPTWhatsApp Integrate ChatGPT for WhatsApp

THE FUTURE OF CHATGPT IN MARKETING

1. **Personalization at scale:** One of the biggest trends in AI marketing is the use of machine learning algorithms to personalise marketing campaigns at scale. This involves using AI to analyse customer data and generate personalised content, offers, and recommendations that are tailored to the specific interests and needs of each individual customer.

2. **Voice and visual search:** Another trend in AI marketing is the use of voice and visual search technologies to enable more natural and intuitive interactions with customers. For example, brands are using AI-powered voice assistants and image recognition algorithms to allow customers to search for products and services using voice or visual queries.

3. **Interactive chatbots:** Chatbots are becoming increasingly sophisticated and are being used in a variety of marketing contexts, such as customer service, lead generation, and content marketing. These chatbots are powered by AI and can hold natural, human-like conversations with customers, providing personalised and efficient service.

4. **Predictive analytics:** AI is also being used to power predictive analytics in marketing, which allows brands to forecast customer behaviour and optimise their marketing efforts accordingly. For example, AI can be used to predict customer churn, identify upsell and cross-sell opportunities, and optimise marketing spend.

5. **AI-generated content:** Finally, AI is being used to generate a wide range of marketing content, including social media posts, email subject lines, and website copy. This allows brands to generate large amounts of high-quality, personalised content in a short amount of time, improving the efficiency and effectiveness of their marketing efforts.

AI technologies will transform marketing in significant ways, and we are only beginning to see the possibilities!

EXAMPLES OF CHATGPT PROMPTS & ANSWERS

Prompt to ChatGPT: Can you build the buyer persona and avatar of my book "The Ultimate B2B Marketing List: 200+ Innovative Tactics you need to try"?

ChatGPT Answers:

Sure, I'd be happy to help you build a buyer persona for your book. A buyer persona is a fictionalised representation of your ideal reader, based on market research and real data about your target audience. An avatar is a specific type of buyer persona that is more focused on the specific characteristics and demographics of an individual reader.

To begin, we'll need to gather some information about your target audience. Here are a few questions to get started:

1. Who is your target reader?
2. What is their job title or role?
3. What are their goals and challenges in their role?
4. What is their education level and industry experience?
5. What are their values and interests outside of work?
6. What type of content or resources do they typically consume?
7. How do they prefer to consume content (e.g., online articles, in-person events, social media)?
8. What motivates them to buy a book like yours?

With this information, we can start to build a detailed picture of your ideal reader and create a buyer persona that reflects their characteristics, goals, and challenges. Once we have a good understanding of your target audience, we can then create an avatar that represents a specific individual within that audience.

Does that make sense? Can you provide some information about your target audience so we can get started?

Follow-Up Prompt: Target audience is B2B Marketing Professionals, B2B C-Suite

Thanks for the information! Based on what you've told me, it sounds like your target reader is a professional who is responsible for B2B marketing within their organisation, or a member of the C-suite who has a strategic role in B2B marketing.

Here are a few potential buyer persona profiles for your book:

1. Sarah is a B2B Marketing Manager at a mid-sized software company. She has a bachelor's degree in Marketing and 5 years of experience in the industry. Sarah is responsible for developing and executing marketing campaigns to generate leads and drive sales. She is always looking for new tactics and strategies to try but has limited time and budget to work with. Sarah consumes content primarily online, through blogs and social media, and is motivated to buy a book like yours if it offers practical, actionable advice that she can implement quickly and effectively.

2. Jack is the Chief Marketing Officer at a large technology firm. He has an MBA and 15 years of experience in B2B marketing. Jack is responsible for setting the overall direction and strategy for the marketing team and is always looking for new ways to drive growth and differentiate the company in the market. He is interested in both tactical and strategic approaches to marketing, and values thought leadership and best practices. Jack tends to prefer in-depth, research-driven content and is willing to invest in resources that will help him stay on the cutting edge of the industry.

3. Emily is the Founder and CEO of a small consulting firm that specialises in B2B marketing services. She has a master's degree in Business Administration and has been in the industry for 10 years. Emily wears many hats in her business, including marketing, and is always looking for ways to improve her marketing efforts and stand out in a crowded market. She values efficiency and practicality and is most likely to purchase a book like yours if it offers clear, step-by-step instructions for implementing new tactics and strategies.

These are just a few examples of potential buyer personas for your book. With more information about your target audience, we can create even more detailed and specific profiles. Do any of these profiles seem particularly relevant to your target reader? Do you have any additional questions or information to add?

Write me the PPT copy for me to promote my book!

Slide 1:

Title: "The Ultimate B2B Marketing List: 200 Tactics You Need to Try"

Slide 2:

Bullet point list of key features or benefits of the book, such as:

- Comprehensive guide to B2B marketing tactics
- Up-to-date and relevant for today's market
- Practical, actionable advice and tips
- Written by a B2B marketing expert

Slide 3:

Title: "What You'll Learn"

- Sub Bullet list of key topics or chapters covered in the book, such as:
- How to generate leads and acquire customers
- Strategies for effective content marketing
- Tips for leveraging social media and email marketing techniques for improving search engine visibility and website traffic

Slide 4:

Title: "About the Author"

Short bio or background information about the author, highlighting their expertise or experience in B2B marketing

Slide 5:

Title: "Praise for The Ultimate B2B Marketing List"

Quotes or reviews from industry experts or satisfied readers, to help build credibility and social proof

Slide 6:

Title: "Where to Buy"

Information on where readers can purchase the book, such as online retailers or bookstores

Slide 7:

Title: "Contact the Author"

Contact information for the author, including a website or social media profiles, to allow readers to connect or learn more about the book.

Can you write me an ad copy for my book "The Ultimate B2B Marketing List: 200 Tactics you need to try" in the style of Breakthrough Advertising by Eugene Schwartz?

Here is an ad copy in the style of Breakthrough Advertising by Eugene Schwartz for your book "The Ultimate B2B List":

"Are you struggling to generate leads and acquire customers in the B2B market? Do you feel like you're constantly falling behind your competitors, no matter how hard you try?

Then you need "The Ultimate B2B List: 200 Tactics You Need to Try." In this comprehensive guide, a B2B marketing expert [Author Name] breaks down the latest trends and techniques for winning in the business-to-business space.

From researching your dream buyers to maximising conversions throughout the sales funnel, this book is packed with practical, actionable advice that you can put into practice right away. Plus, with chapters on topics like content marketing, search engine optimization, and customer stickiness, you'll have everything you need to build a pipeline that consistently delivers results.

Don't miss out on your chance to take your B2B marketing to the next level. Get "The Ultimate B2B List" today and start seeing the results you've always wanted."

What about in the style of Gary Vaynerchuk?

Here is an ad copy in the style of Gary Vaynerchuk for your book "The Ultimate B2B List":

"Hey, [Audience]! Are you tired of the same old B2B marketing strategies that just aren't cutting it anymore? Are you ready to up your game and start seeing real results in your business?

If you answered yes to either of those questions, then you need "The Ultimate B2B List: 200 Tactics You Need to Try" in your life. This book is packed with actionable advice from a B2B marketing expert [Author Name] that will help you dominate the business-to-business space.

From researching your dream buyers to solidifying sales and marketing alignment, this book covers it all. And with chapters on topics like content marketing, search engine optimization, and customer stickiness, you'll have all the tools you need to build a pipeline that delivers results.

Don't miss out on your chance to take your B2B marketing to the next level. Get "The Ultimate B2B List" today and start seeing the results you've always wanted."

Can you convert to bullet points?

- Tired of ineffective B2B marketing strategies?
- Ready to improve your business and see results?
- "The Ultimate B2B List: 200 Tactics You Need to Try" can help!
- Written by B2B marketing expert [Author Name]
- Full of actionable advice on various topics such as:
    - Researching dream buyers
    - Solidifying sales and marketing alignment
    - Content marketing
    - Search engine optimization
    - Customer stickiness

- Take your B2B marketing to the next level
- Get "The Ultimate B2B List" today!

Prompt to ChatGPT: "Generate a list of the top 10 facts, statistics and trends related to B2B Marketing, including their source"

Here are ten potential facts, statistics, and trends related to B2B marketing, along with their sources:

1. B2B marketers are focusing more on content marketing, with 86% of them using it in their marketing strategies (Source: Content Marketing Institute)
2. Email marketing is the most effective channel for B2B marketers, with a median ROI of 122% (Source: Campaign Monitor)
3. B2B e-commerce is expected to reach $1.8 trillion in annual sales by 2023 (Source: Forrester)
4. Video marketing is becoming increasingly popular among B2B brands, with 70% of them using it (Source: Wyzowl)
5. Social media is a key part of the B2B marketing mix, with LinkedIn being the most popular platform (Source: Social Media Examiner)
6. Personalization is important to B2B buyers, with 87% saying it influences their purchasing decisions (Source: Epsilon)
7. Account-based marketing (ABM) is gaining traction in the B2B space, with 70% of companies using it (Source: SiriusDecisions)
8. The majority of B2B buyers (89%) prefer to research products online before making a purchase (Source: Google)
9. B2B companies are investing more in SEO, with 63% saying it has a significant impact on their lead generation (Source: BrightEdge)
10. Influencer marketing is being used by 49% of B2B companies, with LinkedIn being the most popular platform for this (Source: Tomoson)

POWERFUL EXAMPLES OF USING CHATGPT WITH OTHER TOOLS

ChatGPT and SEO.AI:
Quickly Build Blogs that Rank High on Google with Great SEO and Pass AI Detectors

Step 1: Ask ChatGPT to list popular news sites in your niche.

Step 2: Select the category you want to focus on.

Step 3: Copy a selected article and paste it into ChatGPT, then ask it to paraphrase the content.

Step 4: Ask ChatGPT to expand on the details several times until the desired length is reached.

Step 5: Go to SEO.AI and paste in all the content. Have it give you a score. If the score is low, implement the suggestions it gives and copy all the recommendations it gives you.

Step 6: Go back to ChatGPT to include all keywords into the article and rewrite it.

Step 7: Click on search intents and have it generate more relevant content, as well as a title.

Step 8: Once it has a high score, go to Crossplag to check the plagiarism score.

Step 9: Get Quillbot to rewrite the article.

By following these steps, you'll have a blog that ranks high on Google with great SEO and is not detectable as AI-generated content.

ChatGPT and Canva:
Create 10 Social Media Posts in 5 Minutes

Step 1: Get ChatGPT to generate quotes in your niche and target audience.

Step 2: Select the quotes that are relevant, copy them, and save them in Google Sheets as a CSV file.

Step 3: Go to Canva and select your quote card design. Use a template, add your logo and font, and adjust brand colours.

Step 4: In Canva, go to the Apps button at the bottom left corner and type in "bulk" in the search bar. Click bulk create and upload the CSV file.

Step 5: Select the earlier design and right-click "connect data."

Step 6: Click "generate" in Canva and make any necessary adjustments.

There you have it! 10 quote cards for your social media accounts, all created in just 5 minutes using ChatGPT, Google Sheets, and Canva.

PART ONE:

GETTING TO KNOW YOUR DREAM BUYERS

INTRODUCTION

"Get closer than ever to your customer. So close, in fact, that you tell them what they need before they realise it."[5]

Steve Jobs

What is an Ideal Customer Profile (ICP) and why is it Important?

An ideal customer profile (ICP) is a description of your dream buyers – the ones you want more of. These are the customers that consistently buy from the company, share positive experiences with others, and do not churn. They are also the customers who had a specific need that was effectively addressed by the company's value proposition and had a relatively quick and smooth sales process.

When an ICP is well executed, it can help you speed up your sales cycle, gain more customers and increase sales conversions. The ICP helps guide the sales and marketing teams by providing criteria for identifying potential customers that are a good fit for the company's products or services. It should serve as a reference point for these teams as they build the customer base.

While the ICP should not be used to automatically accept or reject all new prospects, it can be used to focus efforts on reaching out to companies that are likely to be interested in your offerings.

---

[5] https://quotefancy.com/quote/911620/Steve-Jobs-Get-closer-than-ever-to-your-customers-So-close-that-you-tell-them-what-they

THREE STEPS TO IDENTIFY AND BUILD YOUR ICP

Identifying the ICP is an important step in developing a go-to-market strategy, as it shapes many of the decisions and actions that follow.

Step One:

First, you can gather data about your target market by analysing your database of existing customers and identifying common characteristics, such as geography, industry, company size, and the people involved in the buying process.

Step Two:

Once you have analysed your customer data, you can use it to create a detailed profile of your ideal customer. This profile should include details such as demographics, needs, pain points, behaviours, and interests.

Step Three:

To bring this profile to life, you can create an avatar for your buyer persona, which should include a name and profile picture, as well as other identifying characteristics that align with your ideal customer profile. Having an avatar for your buyer persona can help you better understand and connect with your target market and create more effective marketing and sales strategies. It can also help you identify potential customers and opportunities in your target market.

A buyer persona is a fictionalised representation of customers. Therefore, it is important to create a customer profile first as it contains information about a group of customers, and then use that information to create a buyer persona.

TIP: Always collaborate with your sales teams when creating an ICP. It gets you in sync with sales, and when the sales and marketing teams align, you are well-positioned to drive conversions and increase revenue.

INNOVATIVE TACTICS TO REFINE YOUR ICP

Meet with Customers Face-to-Face

Above all else, nothing is more valuable than getting information from customers first-hand. Regularly reach out to your top customers and ask them for their input directly.

Invite your top customers, either in a small group setting or on a one-on-one basis to a casual gathering, a lunch/ or dinner, a cocktail hour. Alternatively, online meetings can be an option too.

In your request, you can inform them that you value them as your key customer and would like to interview them to gather insights that will help you improve your research, content, and other deliverables.

You can also be honest and say, you would like to find more customers just like them.

For certain clients who want to remain private, you can assure them that their identities will be kept anonymous by using anonymized names.

Record the interviews. Use a tool like Otter.ai and get transcripts. It'll automatically provide you with the main keywords that are frequently used, and you can also scroll through and capture what's interesting.

> **TIP:** Consider including a small token of appreciation in your survey request to thank participants for their time. This gesture is likely to be appreciated.

Below are the recommended questions to ask your top customers to gain insights for your persona building:

- What prompted you or your team member to reach out/ book a meeting or free consultation with us the first time?

- Before working with us: what were your challenges, concerns and pain points? So, what were you trying to achieve?
- What frustrations did you face to achieve that goal?
- How did these challenges impact you, personally or in your team?
- How would you describe the results of our partnership?
- In your opinion, what are our real benefits and differentiators? What is your favourite benefit?
- What was your buying process like? How did you do your research? How long did it take?
- Who in your team was involved in the buying process?
- Did you speak with any of our existing customers, or sought outside guidance?
- Have you considered competitors? Why did you finally choose us?
- How would you describe our company to others?
- How can we do better?
- What are your upcoming goals with our products and services in the next 3-6 months?
- What content do you like most from us or others out there? What formats do you enjoy (e.g., Infographics, videos, whitepapers, slides etc)?
- What topics do you like to see more of?
- What types of content do you view online and on which channels? Who are your top content creators?
- Are you (and your peers) a part of specific associations or communities? Can you name them? Are you active?

Some people will give generic or short answers and it is your job to probe further with questions like:

- Why was this important to you?
- Can you elaborate further?
- Why did you make this decision

Run an Online Survey

Interviews are typically more effective for gathering detailed and valuable information than surveys, which often elicit short responses. However, if it's difficult to conduct interviews, you can certainly run an online survey instead.

Use a tool like SurveyMonkey to send out an email with a link to the survey and include multiple choice questions where possible. Be sure to read about their Privacy Policies.

To increase participation, consider offering a voucher, gift, or chance to win a prize. The response rate is likely to be higher if you send the email at least twice and someone in your team follows up with them.

> **TIP**: For optimal response rates, ensure that the email request to participate in the survey is sent from a senior executive- such as VP of Marketing, rather than a generic company email address.

To gain valuable insights specific to different demographics, analyse your collected data using a combination of filters such as geography, industry, company size, job titles, and job levels.

Join Sales Calls to Gain Insights from *Potential* Clients

Often overlooked, you can also gain customer insights from potential clients. Work with your sales team and join select sales calls. Listen for their pain points and specific needs. Take note of industry-specific terminology and use it in your marketing materials.

When the opportunity arises, politely ask if you can ask a few questions to better understand them.

Keep in mind that the level of comfort and willingness to share information can vary among potential customers. Tailor the number of questions asked based on the level of relationship and openness. While some may be open to a marketing team member joining the call, others may not be as comfortable. However, in most cases, potential customers will not object to the presence of a marketing team member on the call.

Win/Loss Interviews

Win/Loss Interviews are conducted to gain valuable insights into the success or failure of your sales efforts. This analysis can reveal the reasons behind a customer choosing your product or service, or why they opted not to. Using this feedback to create a report can not only improve your future sales processes but also help you in gaining insights about your ICP and campaign ideas.

While preferably conducted by a third-party expert, these interviews can be done by internal team members as well, as long as they were not directly involved in the opportunity.

Other Sources to Look Out For

There are several sources to gather insights about your customer. Keep an eye for them and note the information down.

- Questions asked by customers & prospects during webinars
- Emails and conversations between your teams and customers
- Comments under your posts/advertisements or those of your competitors
- Public Reviews of you and your competitors
- Discussions in Communities related to the customers line of business or industry/sub industry, global or region / country specific
- Agendas and topics of industry-specific or Line of Business-specific seminars or conferences. These events usually cover current and relevant issues in the field.

KEEP THIS IN MIND:

The Importance of Category Targeting: Appealing to a Larger Market

" **The 95-5 Law**[6] **states that at any given period 95% of potential buyers are not ready to make a purchase today, but will be in the future. This is especially true in B2B.**"
Ty Heath

Director of Market Engagement, B2B Institute at LinkedIn

While focusing on your ideal customer profile (ICP) is an effective way to target a specific segment of the market, it's also important to consider a broader approach known as category targeting or the larger market formula.

This approach involves targeting not only decision makers but also the entire buying spectrum, including champions, influencers, and the C-suite, as well as both larger and smaller companies. This is important because people change jobs and by casting a wide net it can help you capture a larger network of potential influencers and buyers, which is beneficial for the future cash flows and valuation of your company.

The most successful companies can balance their marketing efforts to both the in-market and out-market buyers, and both sales activation and brand building.

---

[6] https://business.linkedin.com/marketing-solutions/b2b-institute/b2b-research/trends/95-5-rule

TOOLS TO HELP YOU IN YOUR BUYER RESEARCH

Make My Persona - Free Buyer Persona Template Generator (2022)

Make My Persona HubSpot is a free tool that helps you create practical customer profiles for every team within the company, specifically by creating buyer personas.

It is especially useful for marketing, but also for sales, customer relationship management, and customer service teams.

It offers a step-by-step customer profile template, with the option to add extra sections for additional customer data. Easy to use, with a user-friendly interface, the tool allows you to pick an avatar and add demographic information.

A fun and visual way to create a persona, but it does have some limitations in the type of data you can add.

AnswerThePublic

AnswerThePublic provides insights into the questions and topics that people are searching for on the internet. It generates a visual representation of common questions, prepositions, and comparisons related to a specific keyword or phrase.

It's very useful for content creators and marketers, and researchers who want to understand what people are interested in and how they are expressing those interests online.

It can help you identify potential gaps in information and generate ideas for new content or campaigns. AnswerThePublic is available as a web-based tool.

BuzzSumo

This tool allows you to analyse and track the performance of content on the web, helping you to discover what content is popular and shared the most on social media in your market. It also provides insights into the content strategies of your competitors, allowing you to search for specific topics or websites and see <u>the most shared content related to those queries</u>.

Additionally, BuzzSumo can be used to identify influencers in your industry and track the performance of your own content.

Google Trends

Google Trends provides marketers with insights about the volume of Google searches for specific topics or search terms, as well as for the geographic locations where these searches are most popular.

It can be accessed in real-time for a specified range of data and can be used for comparative keyword research, finding trends in a particular niche, and more.

Easily identify trending keywords and capture the interests of their buyer personas in a particular topic to optimise website traffic, analyse Search Engine Optimisation (SEO) performance.

Google Trends data is collected from an unbiased sample of search data and can be categorised and clustered to help marketers understand their audience. Google Trends can help B2B marketers boost their omnichannel marketing efforts and improve the overall brand strategy.

PART TWO:

CRAFTING KILLER CONTENT

INTRODUCTION

In 1996, Bill Gates wrote an essay called "Content is King"[7] in which he predicted that content would be a major source of revenue on the internet. Nearly 30 years later, he couldn't be more right!

According to HubSpot[8], 70% of marketers are investing in content marketing, 40% of marketers say that content marketing is a central part of their marketing strategy, and 81% say their company views content as a business strategy. Therefore:

"If you are not writing, posting, promoting, or sharing valuable content, you are actively putting your business at a disadvantage against competition."

Neil Patel[9]

Digital Marketing Expert and Thought Leader

Despite the importance of content for businesses, many struggle with creating original content that resonates with their audience and that they will find valuable.

What is Content Marketing and Why is it Important?

B2B Content Marketing is a method of creating and distributing valuable, relevant, and consistent content to a specific audience with the goal of increasing brand awareness, driving website traffic, generating leads, and ultimately increasing sales.

This is done through various forms of content such as blogs, podcasts, email newsletters, ad copies, infographics, and videos.

---

[7] https://medium.com/@HeathEvans/content-is-king-essay-by-bill-gates-1996-df74552f80d9
[8] https://www.hubspot.com/marketing-statistics
[9] https://neilpatel.com/blog/guide-to-content-marketing/

The third section of this book is specifically dedicated to the use of visuals and videos, which are critical elements of successful content marketing.

Content marketing is an essential strategy for B2B companies because it has a high return on investment (ROI) as shown by data from Statista which states that 30% of marketers consider content to have the highest ROI of any channel[10].

Many B2B marketers also use content marketing to position themselves as thought leaders in their industry, which helps in building trust and credibility with potential customers.

Additionally, according to Brian Dean, the founder of backlink.io, effective content strategies can lead to significant traffic, leads and sales[11]. A good portion of his customers cite his company's content as the reason they decided to purchase from him.

---

[10] https://backlinko.com/hub/content/b2b
[11] https://backlinko.com/hub/content/b2b

FIVE STEPS TO IMPROVE THE EFFECTIVENESS OF YOUR CONTENT STRATEGY

Here are five steps to improve the effectiveness of your content marketing strategy:

Step One:

Create a detailed buyer persona. As highlighted in part one of this book, having an intimate understanding of your buyers will help you create content that speaks to their needs and interests.

Step Two:

Segment your audience for higher open and engagement rates. A survey from Mailchimp found that segmented campaigns had open rates 14.31% higher than non-segmented campaigns[12], and they saw a 101% increase in clicks over non-segmented campaigns. Segmented campaigns also had lower bounce rates, unsubscribes, and instances of spam reporting.

Step Three:

Focus on becoming a thought leader. When done correctly, thought leadership can be very powerful. A LinkedIn study[13] found that 71% of professionals felt that less than half of thought leadership content provided valuable insights. 65% of respondents said that a piece of thought leadership content changed their perception of a company for the better, and 64% said that they believed thought leadership was a more trustworthy source than marketing material. To become a thought leader, focus on what you know and make it great. Remember the Google

---

[12] https://mailchimp.com/en-gb/resources/effects-of-list-segmentation-on-email-marketing-stats/

[13] https://www.edelman.com/expertise/business-marketing/2021-b2b-thought-leadership-impact-studyhip-impact-report

Algorithm acronym EEAT: Experience, Expertise, Authority, and Trust.

Step Four:

Make your content more valuable and shareable. 69% of bloggers use social share buttons[14] on their blog posts to promote their content on social media. To make your content more valuable and shareable, focus on the most attractive aspects of your product or service offering and promote it through social media and other channels.

Step Five:

Find your engine. What part of your product offering is most attractive to your audience? Pay more attention to what drives revenue for your brand and put your energy into promoting and developing those products or services. Don't spread yourself too thin by focusing on supplementary products; instead, put your efforts into what truly makes a difference for your business.

---

[14] https://optinmonster.com/blogging-statistics/

INNOVATIVE TACTICS FOR CONTENT DEVELOPMENT

Let's explore some successful tactics related to content creation and optimization. These tactics include identifying effective ideas for new content, as well as adjusting existing content to enhance its performance.

User-Generated Content

User content, also known as customer-generated content or user-generated content, refers to any form of online media that has been created and published by your customers or users. This can include reviews, ratings, testimonials, social media posts, blog comments, and others.

In B2B marketing, user content can be a powerful way for showcasing the real-world use and benefits of a product or service to potential customers.

By leveraging user content, you can build brand authenticity and trust with your target audience, while also gaining valuable insights into customer needs and preferences.

Whether through social media, customer review platforms, or company blogs, user content can play a key role in attracting and retaining B2B customers.

> **TIP:** Do everything you can to make it easy for your customers to create content about your company. For example, you can offer interview, writing and audio/video development services to assist them.

To drive user generated content, look at these innovative tactics:

- In exchange for a special offer (e.g., product discounts), get the customer to agree on generating a series of content for your brand.

- Highlight your customer in the press: If you work with a PR agency, you can assign them to arrange an interview with one of your customers to highlight the customer's success with your product. It can be very good exposure for the customer as the piece can focus on the customer's priorities; for example, showcasing their focus on product quality or customer service with your products and services.
- Run a user-generated content contest or challenge. Offer a prize for the best customer-submitted photo, review, or testimonial. Promote the contest through social media, email marketing, and your website.
- Partner with influencers in your industry. Collaborate with influencers to create user-generated content about your company or products.

Once you have generated user content (photos, reviews, testimonials, news coverage), aggressively use them on your content channels : websites, social media, emails and newsletters, and even banners for events. User content can also be powerful to use in your ads.

Evergreen Content

Evergreen content is a type of content that can engage and educate readers over a long period of time, without requiring a lot of extra effort. By mastering the skill of creating "timeless" content, you can ensure that your articles, e-books, and tutorials remain relevant and useful for years to come.

Some examples of evergreen content in the B2B space might include:

- A Buyers Guide
- Tips & Tricks
- Playbooks, Frameworks or Checklists
- How-to Guides
- Listicles
- An Impact Report
- Executive Authorship
- Content to Win Against Competition

There are many benefits to creating evergreen content, including increased traffic, improved search engine optimization (SEO), higher brand awareness, and greater credibility.

> **TIP:** To write effective evergreen content, it's important to select topics that have the potential to consistently generate traffic. Analytical tools or keywords tools as outlined in the book can help you identify these types of topics, which are characterised by attracting a high volume of traffic initially and maintaining a steady level of traffic over time.
>
> After selecting your topics, it is important to use relevant keywords in your content to increase the chances of it appearing in search results. Additionally, it is important to avoid using specific events and dates in your content as it can quickly make it out of date and shorten its lifespan. Even though evergreen content is meant to be timeless, it is still important to update it occasionally to keep it relevant.

Let's look at the several types of evergreen content in more detail:

A Buyers' Guide

A buyer's guide is a document that provides detailed information about a specific product or product category to help potential buyers make informed purchasing decisions.

In the context of B2B marketing, a buyer's guide can be a powerful tool for attracting and engaging potential customers, as it can help them understand the considerations they need to make, the steps they need to undertake, the features and benefits of different products, compare them to similar products on the market, and ultimately make a purchase decision that aligns with their business needs.

> **TIP:** Address all of the queries and concerns a potential customer may have while searching for the most suitable solution for their requirements. It is essential to present the information in an objective manner and avoid being overly promotional, as this can quickly erode credibility.

Playbooks, Frameworks or Checklists

Playbooks, frameworks, or checklists can be useful tools for helping prospects understand and make the most of your product or service.

They educate potential buyers, demonstrate expertise, and build customer loyalty.

How-to Guides

How-to guides are designed to provide step-by-step instructions on how to complete a specific task or solve a particular problem. By offering this type of information, you can demonstrate your expertise and build trust with your audience.

They are practical and useful, designed to be actionable and provide readers with information they can use right away. This makes them particularly appealing to busy professionals who are looking for solutions to their challenges.

They can drive traffic to your website and potentially generate leads.

And finally, they can improve SEO if optimised for relevant keywords driving organic traffic.

> **TIP:** Do not mistake how-to guides with user manuals. A how-to guide is often used to attract new customers and generate leads for a business. Its purpose is to educate potential customers about a product or service and provide them with information that can help them make a purchasing decision. On the other hand, the user manual is meant for people who have already made a purchase, it is designed to provide them with step-by-step instructions on how to use the product effectively. It often concentrates on technical aspects of the product, and it's more of a product-related material.

Listicles

A listicle is a type of article that combines the format of a list with an article. The name "listicle" is a combination of "list" and "article."

They usually consist of an introduction, a series of points or items related to the topic, short explanations, or descriptions of each item, and can include images.

Examples include a list of tools or a list of actionable steps.

Here is a great case study of how Zapier uses Listicles[15] to drive 5 million sessions!

> **TIP:** Listicles are a good opportunity to create "10x content", meaning content that is ten times better than what your competitors have. For example, if a competitor writes a list of "top 15 content marketing tools", you can quickly write a list of "top 35 content marketing tools" and surpass the value of their content. Even if some of the items in your list are the same as in theirs, the additional unique items that you included will significantly increase the value of your post.

An Impact Report

Publishing an impact report is an important part of B2B marketing as it helps to showcase the tangible benefits that customers have gained from using your products and services. By highlighting both quantitative and qualitative data, you can provide a well-rounded view of the value and ROI that your company has brought to your customers.

In addition to featuring the specific results and metrics that demonstrate the impact of your products and services, it's also valuable to include quotes and testimonials from top customers. This helps to provide a more human perspective on the value that you've delivered and adds credibility to the report.

An impact report is a powerful tool for demonstrating the value that your company brings to its customers and for differentiating yourself from competitors. It can be used in a variety of contexts, such as in sales and marketing materials or on your website.

---

[15] https://foundationinc.co/lab/zapier-listicles-seo

Executive Authorship

WARNING: This is a high effort endeavour. Run this only if the senior executive as the designated author understands and is willing to commit to the investment in time and effort.

Publishing an actual book on a related subject matter can be very powerful for several reasons.

First, writing a book establishes the author (for example, your senior executive) as an expert in the field. It demonstrates a deep understanding of the subject matter and a willingness to share this knowledge with others, which can help build credibility and trust with potential clients.

Second, a book can serve as a powerful marketing tool. It can be used to showcase your company's expertise and promote your business to potential clients, while also providing an opportunity to highlight your products or services.

Third, a book can be a powerful lead generation tool. By offering it as a free resource or as a gift in exchange for contact information/ a meeting/ event attendance or so, you can create new business opportunities and nurture leads into paying customers.

Fourth, publishing a book can increase brand awareness and visibility to new avenues, for example at Amazon, Kindle or other Book Repositories, helping to expand your online presence

Bonus benefit: Your senior executive will not soon forget you have made him or her into a published author!

TIP: While writing a book may seem intimidating, you can make the process lighter:

- With the help of a ghost-writer who is knowledgeable in your field. Simply provide the structure and main points you want to convey (written by or approved by your senior executive).

- Print and publish the book via platforms like Amazon Kindle Direct Publishing or ulu.com. (You can choose to sell it and make some change!)

Once a book is completed, it becomes a great source for blogs, and other content for a long time to come. One might argue it is a worthwhile investment!

Brand Defence Content

A brand defence content can be a powerful evergreen content type. To make it easier for potential customers to choose you over competitors, consider creating a comparison table. This table should highlight the key features and differences between your product and its main competitors. By clearly demonstrating where you excel, you can make the choice easier for visitors. This technique can be particularly effective on pricing pages, or on blogs, or as an asset

It can also help you to protect your brand and prevent other companies from ranking for your company's name or products, consider creating a comparison page that showcases your product and its features in comparison to your competitors. This can help defend your brand and prevent others from stealing traffic that is meant for your company.

> **TIP:** To enhance credibility, include a few minor points where your competitors have an advantage, as this can make the comparison seem less biased.

Powerful Content Types that are not Evergreen:

Content that is not considered evergreen includes responses to recent political events, references to memes and fads, and predictions about future trends. While this type of content can be effective, it's important to ensure that it doesn't make up most of your content strategy. Instead, it's crucial to strike a balance between evergreen and timely content.

You can use non-evergreen content strategically. Below are two highly effective examples.

Industry Studies

Industry studies can be the most effective type of B2B content that can be created. A great example is an Industry Study published by Backlinko:

We analysed 5.2 Million Desktop and Mobile Pages, Here is What We Learned About Page Speed[16]

They published this page loading speed industry study on their blog and it brought in 59,653 visitors, shared on social media 4002 times and 675 websites linked to that study.

The real benefit of industry studies is the number of backlinks they generate which is important for Search Engine Optimisation (SEO).

Industry studies can also help establish the author or the company as a thought leader in their industry.

> **TIP:** Publish the findings of industry studies as freely available articles or blog posts, as opposed to gating it, as this increases the chances of it being shared and linked to. Additionally, be transparent about the methodology of the study, by providing a PDF link to the methods and linking to a GitHub repository with the raw data, this way it can be easily reproduced and verified by others.

Proprietary Research Reports

Similarly, creating proprietary research reports is also a highly effective form of B2B content marketing. Two great examples of this are Salesforce's Annual State of Marketing report[17] and Upwork's Future Workforce Report[18].

The Salesforce report, which has been published for eight consecutive years, provides insights on the changing trends, priorities, and challenges in the marketing industry. The report is based on data from 6000 global marketers and trillions of outbound marketing messages, making it a highly reputable and reliable source of information for marketing professionals.

In addition to being a valuable resource, the Salesforce report is also a versatile form of content. The company repurposes the report into various formats, such as a landing page, email campaign, social media

---

[16] https://backlinko.com/page-speed-stats
[17] https://www.salesforce.com/resources/research-reports/state-of-marketing/
[18] https://www.upwork.com/i/future-workforce/fw/2020/

posts, and blog highlights, giving them endless content options. By breaking down the report into different segments, they can target specific audiences with tailored messages.

Creating proprietary research reports like these can help establish your company as an authority in your industry. It's worth investing the time and effort to create valuable content like this. While it may be challenging the first time, subsequent years will require less effort. By analysing the strategies and frameworks used by other companies, such as Salesforce, you can reverse-engineer and adapt them to create your own successful research report campaign.

> **TIP:** As with Industry Studies, publish the key findings of your Proprietary Research Reports as freely as possible and be transparent about the methodology.

Content to Empower Sales

Sales Plays

A Sales Play is a specific approach to selling a solution to a particular group of customers and personas, which is designed to be used repeatedly by a sales team or channel partner. It includes a specific market and sales offering, as well as a sales strategy, and is intended to be effective during a specific period.

Bain defines sales plays as "the golden thread that connects strategy and execution."[19]

Sales plays are a key element in successful selling as they make it easier for both the seller and buyer. Companies that use sales plays tend to have higher win rates and teams that track them effectively see even higher success rates.

To create effective sales plays, product marketers and enablement teams should use data-informed guidance on the best course of action to win an opportunity with a specific prospect. To ensure maximum impact, it is important that the sales plays are easy to adopt, include all necessary assets and tools in one place, provide real examples of top performers in

---

[19]

action, and are easily accessible to the sales team.

Content for Prospects to Make the Case to Superiors

Assist employees in making the case to their superiors to invest in your product. Oftentimes, individuals evaluating your product may not have the authority to make a purchase. To aid them in their efforts, provide them with pre-written email templates, slides or infographics that clearly communicate the positive impact your product will have on the company's overall performance. This is the key information that decision-makers are most interested in. A simple example of such a content of this can be found here:

https://conversionxl.com/institute/reimbursement/

AD CONTENT BUILDING TACTICS

B2B advertising differs from B2C advertising in various ways and therefore requires a different approach.

B2B advertising platforms are typically more advanced than B2C platforms and B2B digital marketing tends to be more comprehensive.

Research shows that B2B customers spend more time researching products (Read: The Four Must-Know Trends in B2B Marketing: The Self-Service Buyer) and focus more on the details.

The best B2B ads are typically at the top of the sales funnel. To be effective, B2B advertising platforms must be able to track customers throughout the sales funnel and guide them towards a decision.

B2B paid advertising campaigns should target decision makers and influencers. The best B2B campaigns engage customers at multiple levels of the marketing process, over time.

B2B companies often advertise on multiple platforms and use analytics to determine the most effective strategies and audiences.

Let's go through some tactics:

Find Inspiration from Copygenius.io

Copygenius.io helps businesses find B2B ad targeting ideas. It works by analysing successful ad campaigns and extracting the key elements that contributed to their success. This includes identifying common themes, messaging, and targeting strategies used in the campaigns.

Using Copygenius.io, you can generate ideas for targeting specific industry sectors, job titles, or demographics. The tool also provides suggestions for ad copy and messaging that resonates with the target audience.

One way that businesses can use Copygenius.io is by inputting their own target audience and industry to see what ad campaigns have been successful in similar situations. They can then use this information to inform their own ad targeting strategy and create more effective campaigns.

The Best Ad Doesn't Look Like an Ad

The best way to advertise is to not make it look like an advertisement. One way is to educate your target audience within their news feed. Instead of simply trying to get clicks, use your expertise and unique perspective to teach your audience something valuable. In your ad text, which should be a short LinkedIn post of around 600 characters, use clear, short, and simple sentences to ensure high readability.

Try to structure each paragraph as two or three lines. To make your ad catchier, include a title of around 200 characters that mentions a benefit, problem, frustration, or common mistake that your audience may be experiencing.

When crafting your ad, think about how you can communicate the maximum amount of relevant and valuable information to your audience, even if they don't click on the ad.

The Anti-Ad Copy

Still related to the previous point, as a B2B marketer, you may want to try an "anti-ad" approach in your copywriting. This means writing copy that goes against traditional ad conventions and instead focuses on honesty, transparency, and authenticity.

Here are a few reasons why B2B marketers should consider trying the anti-ad copy approach:

1. It helps to build trust: By being transparent and honest in your copy, you can build trust with your audience and establish yourself as a reliable and credible source of information.

2. It differentiates you from competitors: In a crowded and competitive market, standing out is key. By taking an anti-ad approach, you can differentiate yourself from competitors and stand out in the minds of your audience.

3. It resonates with modern consumers: Modern consumers are savvy

and increasingly sceptical of traditional advertising. By taking an anti-ad approach, you can appeal to their desire for authenticity and honesty.

4. It can be more effective: By not trying to sell your product or service too hard, you can make your message more effective. By focusing on the value and benefits of your product or service, you can build a stronger case for why your audience should choose you.

B2B marketers should try the anti-ad copy approach to appeal to modern consumers. By being transparent and authentic in your messaging, you can effectively convey the value of your product or service and drive conversions.

Here are some examples: of the anti-ad copy:

"We're not perfect, but we're always improving"

> This type of copy acknowledges that no company or product is perfect, but that you are committed to constantly improving. This can help to build trust with your audience and show that you are transparent and willing to listen to feedback.

"We don't have all the answers, but we're working on it"

> This type of copy acknowledges that you may not have all the answers, but that you are actively working to find them. This can show your audience that you are open to learning and willing to take on new challenges.

"We may not be the cheapest, but we're worth the investment"

> This type of copy acknowledges that you may not be the cheapest option on the market, but that the value and quality of your product or service make it worth the investment. This can help to position your brand as a premium offering and set you apart from competitors.

"We're not trying to sell you anything, we just want to help"

> This type of copy downplays the sales aspect of your marketing efforts and instead focuses on the value and benefits of your product or service. By showing that you are genuinely interested in helping your audience, you can build trust and credibility.

Storytelling

Storytelling has long been a powerful tool for engaging and influencing audiences. In the world of B2B advertising, this is no different. By incorporating storytelling techniques into your ad campaigns, you can effectively convey your message and differentiate your brand from competitors.

One of the key benefits of using storytelling in B2B ads is that it helps to humanise your brand. Rather than simply presenting a list of features and benefits, storytelling allows you to connect with your audience on an emotional level and showcase the value that your product or service brings to their lives.

Another advantage of using storytelling in B2B advertising is that it helps to build trust and credibility with your audience. By sharing real-life examples and case studies, you can demonstrate the effectiveness of your product or service and build confidence in your brand.

Moreover, storytelling can also help to make your ad campaigns more memorable. By creating a compelling narrative that resonates with your audience, you can increase the chances that your message will stick in their minds and drive future conversions.

The power of storytelling in B2B advertising lies in its ability to engage and connect with your audience on a deeper level. By incorporating storytelling techniques into your ad campaigns, you can effectively convey your message, build trust and credibility, and drive conversions.

There are several strategies you can use when incorporating storytelling into your B2B ad copy:

1. **Start with a strong opening:** Hook your audience's attention with an engaging opening that sets the stage for your story. This could be a question, a quote, or a statistic that resonates with your audience.

2. **Use real-life examples and case studies:** Share real-life examples and case studies to demonstrate the effectiveness of your product or service. This helps to build credibility and authenticity with your audience.

3. **Use relatable characters:** People are more likely to connect with stories that feature relatable characters. Consider using customer testimonials or case studies that feature people like your target

audience.

4. **Create a clear and compelling narrative:** A clear and compelling narrative helps to guide your audience through your story and keeps them engaged. Make sure to include a beginning, middle, and end to your story.

5. **Include a call to action:** End your story with a strong call to action that encourages your audience to take the next step, whether it's visiting your website, signing up for a trial, or making a purchase.

By following these strategies, you can effectively incorporate storytelling into your B2B ad copy and engage your audience in a meaningful way.

Highly Personalised Content

LinkedIn's ad as well as Google Ad targeting allows you to create highly personalised content for your ads, based on the specific audience you are targeting.

For example, if you are targeting CEOs at medical companies or very specific keywords related to a vertical and role, you can create a copy that speaks directly to this audience and addresses their specific needs and concerns.

By creating a content or copy that is highly relevant to your target audience, you can increase the chances that they will click on your ad and engage with your content. This can help to improve your ad's click-through rate (CTR) and drive more qualified traffic to your website.

CONTENT BUILDING TECHNIQUES

Use "Even if" Statements

Address and remove potential objections that readers may have by using the "even if" technique in your copywriting.

This involves presenting your product or service as capable of achieving a desirable outcome, even in the face of certain objections or challenges. By acknowledging these objections and demonstrating that your product can handle them, you can build trust with readers and differentiate yourself from competitors who may not address these concerns.

For example, you might say "Build effective automations even if you can't code" to show that your product can be used by anyone, regardless of their coding skills.

Incorporate Customer Feedback and Reviews

Highlighting positive customer experiences can be a powerful way to build trust and credibility with your target audience.

Consider getting the feedback directly or visiting review sites where you collect customer reviews. You should incorporate some of the most well-written and descriptive phrases into your marketing materials.

Often, your users will have a unique and valuable perspective on the benefits and uses of your product, so including their words can add credibility and authenticity to your marketing efforts.

Leverage Internal Experts

Your internal executives likely have valuable insights and expertise that can be shared with your audience through thought leadership content such as blog posts, webinars, and podcasts.

If you're targeting CIOs or CMOs, for example, have your CIO or CMO publish an article or create a piece of content that addresses the challenges and opportunities faced by their peers. This not only helps to authentically position your company as a thought leader, but also allows your executives to share their expertise and insights with a wider audience.

Use headlines or subject lines like "From CIO to CIO", "From one CMO to another" or something similar. This approach can be particularly effective but It's important to remember that personalised and targeted messaging is always key to successful B2B email campaigns.

By using this approach and focusing on the specific needs and interests of your target audience, you can increase the chances that your email will be well received and lead to meaningful engagement with potential clients.

Newsjacking

Stay current on industry trends and topics by keeping an eye on new, exciting, and trending topics related to your business. Sometimes referred to as "newsjacking," you insert your ideas into a breaking news story to attract attention and increase the visibility of your ideas and website.

However, it's important to remember to not exploit or manipulate the news in any way.

Along with that, it's also important to have a good balance of evergreen content that will give you the biggest bang for your buck.

Keep following industry-specific news outlets, blogs, social media channels, and online communities to stay updated on the latest trends and news.

> **TIP:** Use <u>Exploding Topics</u> to find trending topics before they take off, giving you a fantastic edge.

The Four Walls Technique

A part of the storytelling technique, the Four Walls copy technique is a way of creating a marketing message that guides the reader through a series of questions, each of which leads logically to the next, until they are almost ready to make a purchase.

The goal is to "box in" the reader and encourage them to take a stand and make a commitment to their decision. To use this technique, you would pose four questions to your prospect, with each answer leading to the next. For example:

> "Do you enjoy spending hours scouring the web for potential clients?
>
> "Don't you wish there was a better solution to this?
>
> "A tool where you'd simply select the criteria, and you'd get hundreds of quality contacts in a matter of seconds?
>
> "How much would your business grow if you had such a tool?"

Then, at the end of the ad, you would introduce the product or service that you are promoting (in this case, "tool X") and provide a call to action, inviting the reader to take the next step.

This is a perfect example of commitment & consistency bias at play - if you take a stand on an issue, you must remain consistent with your beliefs.

This technique can be effective in persuading readers to act and even make a purchase, but it's important to use it ethically and transparently, and to make sure that the product or service being promoted is actually able to deliver on its promised benefits.

Before and After Examples

Before and after content shows the difference in a product or service before and after it is used.

Studies have shown these types of campaigns consistently increased sales.

This is because they appeal to two main drivers of persuasion:

- people's current pain or dissatisfaction with their current situation, and
- their desire for a better outcome.

For example, a company might show how much time and money they saved by using a certain tool, or how a product improved the appearance or function of something.

Problem Solving Content

To drive targeted traffic and demonstrate your expertise in your niche, consider writing content that focuses on problem-solving. Think about the tools and resources that you use in your work and the potential issues that users may encounter when using them.

By creating helpful content that explains how to overcome these challenges, you can attract an audience that is specifically interested in your area of expertise and provide value to your readers. This type of content can also help to establish you as a thought leader in your field and position your business as a reliable source of information and solutions.

Tailor Your Content to the Customers' CRM stage

This technique will help to ensure that the content you're providing is relevant and valuable to the buyer at each stage of their journey.

One way to do this is to create a dynamic custom audience based on the current stage of the CRM deal for each prospect. Then, create separate campaigns for users at each stage and align the offers in the ads accordingly. This can help ensure that the ads you are running are tailored to the specific needs and interests of your prospects, which can help increase their effectiveness.

Testimonial Carousels

When trying to convert users who are already familiar with your product, consider using testimonials and case studies in your retargeting campaigns. The carousel format, where each card showcases a different case study or testimonial, can be particularly effective for this purpose.

For example, you could create a carousel ad that features case studies from different industries, highlighting the diverse ways in which your product has helped solve problems for a variety of users.

By showcasing real-world examples of your product's effectiveness through testimonials and case studies, you can give users that final push they need to convert and become customers.

Sequential Content

Sequential campaigns involve showing a series of ads to a particular user in a specific order over a set number of days. If a user converts, they are removed from the rest of the sequence. Each ad in the sequence can highlight a different aspect or feature of the product, such as a use case or unique selling point.

For example, if a user visited a landing page but did not sign up for a free trial, a business could set up a Facebook campaign consisting of four ads that are shown one after another, each for three days.

To create a custom audience for each ad, the business could use visitors to the landing page from the previous number of days specified, with those who have already converted being excluded.

This approach can help businesses effectively market their products to potential customers and increase conversions.

IMPROVE YOUR EXISTING CONTENT

Update Old Blogs by 10%

By updating and republishing old blog content, you can not only improve its relevance and accuracy, but also potentially increase your organic click-through rate (CTR) on search engine results pages (SERPs). This is because Google may display the updated publication date if the content has been changed by at least 10%. Additionally, Google tends to favour fresh content, so updating your old content may also give it a slight SEO boost.

Add Current Year to Your Blog Posts

To increase the click-through rate (CTR) from the search results page, you can add the current year to the title of your blog posts. This will make the title appear more relevant and up to date. For example, you could use titles like "How much does it cost to organise a conference in 2023?" or "Google Ads benchmarks [updated for 2023]." This tactic can help you to attract more clicks and potentially drive more traffic to your website.

Optimise your Headlines with Headline Analysers

Headlines are important in all your content because they are the first thing that readers see and can significantly impact their decision to continue reading or to move on.

> "On average, five times as many people read the headline as read the body copy. When you have written your headline, you have spent eighty cents out of your dollar."[20]
>
> David Ogilvy
>
> the Father of Advertising and arguably one of
>
> the best copywriters who ever lived

---

[20] https://www.brainyquote.com/quotes/david_ogilvy_103069

A good headline should be attention-grabbing, relevant, and informative, and should accurately reflect the content that follows. Headlines should also always be search engine optimised.

> **TIP:** Maximise your headlines' impact with these powerful headline analysis tools. One of my favourites is the free headline analyser from coschedule.com .
>
> There are also other great options like Sharethrough, AMI, and TweakYourBiz. Use these tools to analyse all of your past blog headlines and other assets and make adjustments based on the results to improve their performance. As a best practice, make it a standard operating procedure to always run your headlines through these analysis tools before publishing them.

Incorporate Numbers in Your Headline

You can easily boost the impact of your headlines with this simple yet effective tip. As I learned from Sabry Suby's book "Sell like Crazy"[21], incorporating numbers in headlines is a powerful way to grab people's attention.

Whether it's a blog post, whitepaper, or webinar, adding a numerical value will spark interest and signal to the reader that the content is organised and easy to consume. It can also be used to provide clear step-by-step instructions, such as "5 Simple Ways to Increase Staff Engagement" or even "7 Proven Strategies to Boost your Sales" or to share a list like the title of this book illustrates. Make this a regular practice and see the difference it can make in your readership.

Merge Two Pieces of Content

One way to improve the performance of your content and increase organic traffic is to merge two (or more) average-performing pieces of content into one.

---

[21] Suby, S. (2019). Sell Like Crazy: How to Make Insane Money and Build a Business You Love. SellLikeCrazyBook.com.

This works because the page authority of the merged pages is combined into one, which can help improve the overall ranking of the resulting article. Google prefers content that is more than 1000 words. Additionally, the resulting article is often more comprehensive, as it contains information from multiple sources. To do this, you can use a 301 redirect to point users from the lower-authority page to the higher-authority page.

This will help ensure that the combined page receives all the traffic and benefits from the improved page authority. By merging two pieces of content, you can create a more comprehensive and authoritative resource that is more likely to rank well in search results.

Conduct Content Upgrades

Content upgrades can be an impactful way for increasing the conversion rate from blog readers. These upgrades can include resources such as eBooks, checklists, cheat sheets, and swipe files, basically anything that offers additional value to readers by providing additional information or resources related to a specific blog post.

To effectively use content upgrades, it's important to ensure that they are highly relevant to the given blog post and offer extra value that was not included in the article. To maximise the effectiveness of content upgrades, consider displaying them within the content of the blog post and highlighting their relevance and value to readers. By offering valuable content upgrades, you can help to increase the conversion rate from your blog readers and provide them with additional value in return for their engagement.

Repurpose Your Content

To reach more people, you really should be repurposing the content you already have. Try breaking it down and distributing it on different channels. For example, you could turn your best performing text content into videos, audio recordings, slides, or infographics.

Alternatively, you could take your video or audio content and turn it into written or visual formats. If you have a whitepaper that covers 15 customer insights, for example, you could create 15 separate posts each covering one insight or partial paper excerpts and post them on LinkedIn or Twitter. This will allow you to share your content with a wider audience and get more engagement. Best of all, it also saves you plenty of time

> **TIP:** Repurpose.io can help you repurpose content easily, by allowing you to reuse your existing content across different channels and platforms.
>
> With Repurpose.io, you can turn blog posts, podcasts, webinars, and other types of content into social media posts, email newsletters, and even videos, all with just a few clicks. This not only saves you the time and effort of creating new content from scratch, but also helps you reach a wider audience and get more value out of your existing content. In addition, Repurpose.io allows you to schedule and automate your content distribution.

Example of repurposing Content: Turn Your Top Performing Blog into an eBook

One way to repurpose your top performing blog post and reach a wider audience is to turn it into an eBook. An eBook is a digital book that can be downloaded and read on a variety of devices, such as a computer, tablet, or e-reader. By converting your top performing blog post into an eBook, you can leverage the popularity and success of that post and reach a larger audience.

To create an eBook from your blog post, you will need to do the following:

1. **Choose your top performing post:** Identify which of your blog posts has received the most traffic or engagement and consider turning that post into an eBook.

2. **Edit and expand the content:** Edit and expand the content of your blog post to make it more comprehensive and in-depth. Consider adding additional information, examples, or case studies to make the eBook more valuable to readers. (Note: You can always hire writers/content developers for this!)

3. **Design a cover and layout:** Design a cover and layout for your

eBook that is visually appealing and professional. You can use a tool like Canva or Adobe InDesign to create a cover and layout that is consistent with your brand.

4. **Format and publish the eBook:** Format the eBook in a file format that is compatible with e-readers and other devices, such as EPUB or MOBI. You can use a tool like Calibre to convert your eBook to the appropriate file format. Once your eBook is formatted and ready to go, you can publish it on your resources page (gated) or publish it on platforms like Amazon Kindle Direct Publishing or Smashwords.

KEEP THIS IN MIND

Build Content for Every Stage of the Buying Journey

Creating content that aligns with each stage of the buyer's journey is a great way to effectively connect with your target audience. By understanding your buyer persona and how prospects move through the purchasing process, you can create tailored content for each stage and distribute it through the appropriate channels.

While the way that prospects and customers consume content may not always be linear, it is important to have content available for every stage of the journey. This can help you map your content to the relevant stages of the buyer's journey, creating a marketing funnel.

The marketing funnel typically includes three (plus one) phases:

Awareness (Top of the Funnel) when people are looking for information and resources. Common content types are blogs, reports, guides, how-to content. At this stage is where marketers should develop the highest number of contents.

Evaluation/Consideration (Middle of the Funnel) when they are determining if your product or service is a good fit. Common content types include buyer guides, competitive comparison, case studies, product spec.

Conversion/Decision (Bottom of the Funnel) when they are figuring out how to become a customer. Common content types are pricing, demo, consultation, value engineering.

and **Delight/Retention**, when they are using your product. Content types here include customer best practices, manuals, benchmark reports, and top of the funnel content types.

TOOLS FOR CONTENT DEVELOPMENT

Content Research Tools:

AnswerThePublic
BuzzSumo
Google Trends

Keyword Research Tools:

Free Keyword Generator Tool: Find 100+ Keyword Ideas in Seconds
Keyword Generator by Semrush
SEODataViz
Seed Keywords
Google Autocomplete

Copywriting Tools:

ChatGPT: Optimising Language Models for Dialogue
please refer to the BONUS Guide

QuillBot
Unlike ChatGPT, Quillbot is an artificial intelligence tool specifically designed for paraphrasing. If you find content that you believe will benefit your business, you can easily paraphrase it with Quillbot, thereby

making it your own, quickly.

It can also help you improve the quality of your writing by suggesting edits, finding synonyms, and enhancing clarity and meaning. It can also help users integrate vocabulary enhancements into their writing and integrate directly into Microsoft Office, Google Docs, and Google Chrome.

Quillbot is trusted by millions of users worldwide and offers a premium version with additional features and paraphrasing modes. It is designed to save time and improve the clarity and effectiveness of writing by using state-of-the-art AI to rewrite sentences, paragraphs, or articles. Btw, you can use Quillbot and ChatGPT together. Using Quillbot, you can make the content from ChatGPT close to 100% human.

Hemingway Editor

The Hemingway Editor is a writing tool designed to help you improve the clarity and simplicity of your writing. It accomplishes this by highlighting complex sentences and long, dense blocks of text, and by providing suggestions for making your writing more concise and readable.

One of the key features of the Hemingway Editor is its ability to identify areas of your writing that may be difficult for readers to understand or follow. It does this by highlighting complex sentences and long, dense blocks of text, and by providing suggestions for breaking them up or simplifying them. This can be particularly helpful if you're writing for a general audience or for readers who may not be familiar with your subject matter.

In addition to improving the clarity of your writing, the Hemingway Editor also provides a readability score that shows the level of difficulty of your text. This can be useful if you want to ensure that your writing is appropriate for your intended audience. For example, if you're writing for a general audience, you may want to aim for a score of around grade 6 or 7.

Finally, the Hemingway Editor allows you to save your edited text and export it as a PDF or Word document. This can be convenient if you want to share your edited text with others, or if you want to keep a record of your changes. The Hemingway Editor is a useful tool for anyone who wants to improve the clarity and simplicity of their writing.

PART THREE:

MAKING A VISUAL IMPACT

This section, which still pertains to content, is divided into two categories: Visuals and Videos. We'll begin by discussing the power and potential of visual content, including formats such as images, infographics, and charts.

VISUALS

INTRODUCTION

B2B marketers can stay data-driven and professional in their content while bringing in the emotional appeal that marks the best of B2C visuals. This will make your content stand out from the rest.

> "When people hear information, they're likely to remember only 10% of that information three days later. However, if a relevant image is paired with that same information, people retain 65% of the information three days later."[22]
>
> BrainRules

Visual content is such an important element of marketing. It makes your content not just more engaging but also more effectively captures the attention of audiences compared to text alone.

Just look at the growth of image-focused platforms such as Pinterest and Instagram, and you will understand how important visuals are.

When you include visual elements in your marketing materials, you can more effectively communicate your message, drive engagement and: research suggests that people tend to remember information better when it is presented with visuals.

Therefore, B2B marketers should really add visual content into their marketing strategy to support and enhance text-based content.

TYPES OF VISUALS FOR B2B

Search-engine-optimised Charts and Graphs

B2B buyers often prefer content that is data-oriented and includes data visualisations such as charts and graphs. These types of images are particularly effective when optimised for search engines and are most

---

[22] http://brainrules.net/vision/

useful when they provide context and help to tell a story using data. One study found that blog posts with charts and graphs received 258% more trackbacks[23] than posts with other types of images.

Illustrations

For B2B companies, it is advisable to use illustrations, particularly hand-drawn ones, in marketing materials. Illustrations in a clean, flat design are commonly used by B2B SaaS companies in their homepages. Computer-generated illustrations can also be used in B2B content marketing. Hand-drawn illustrations help content stand out and establish your brand, even if it is just a blog post header image shared on social media. Hand-drawn illustrations can help your content stand out and establish your brand, even when used in small ways such as the header image on a blog post shared on social media.

"Real" Photographs

Real photographs, which are taken by employees and capture the company's work environment and culture, can be more effective than traditional, professionally taken photographs or stock photos for B2B visual content.

These photographs may be more casual and resemble social media photos taken for personal accounts, which is seen as more authentic, can pique the interest of B2B buyers and lead them to engage with the content.

Real photographs can be used in company banners and marketing messages, and do not need to be perfect in terms of lighting and angles to be effective. Using real employees in these photographs can also be motivating for the team.

Scroll Triggered Animations

Scroll-triggered animations, also known as "parallax ", animations, can be used to make content on a product features page or a company's home page more dynamic and engaging. An example of this type of animation

---

[23] https://contentmarketinginstitute.com/articles/blog-attractive-visuals/

is Google's "How Search Works" page, which includes headlines, summary text, links, and animations that illustrate different aspects of how search works.

These animations can be created by skilled developers and designers, or with the use of WordPress plugins like Scroll Triggered Animations. However, it is important to ensure that the animations are effective at communicating information and work well on different devices and platforms.

Micro Infographics

Micro-infographics are a type of visual content that are smaller in size than traditional infographics and are a good way to repurpose text-based content. To create a micro-infographic, you can select a few of your best-performing blog posts, choose 5-10 key facts, sentences, or statistics from each post, and ask a designer to turn the text into visually appealing information.

These micro-infographics can be used for social media posts and can also be added to the original blog posts. They are concise, impactful, and convey important information quickly.

Infographics

Infographics are a useful type of visual content that can be created by repurposing existing content, such as a detailed blog post, eBook, or research study, or as a standalone project. They are particularly effective for presenting information in a series of statistics that tell a story or show the state of an industry. Infographics can also be divided into micro-infographics and shared on social media platforms like LinkedIn.

Interactive Infographics

One way to enhance the standard infographic is to allow the user to interact with it in various ways, such as dragging bars, clicking charts, or adjusting the view year by year. This not only increases the time that the user spends on the page, but also allows them to customise the infographic to show the content that they are most interested in. This added level of interaction can make the content more engaging and personalised.

Images of Hand-written Quotes or Other Texts

Hand-written quotes or other text on social media can be an effective way to capture attention and stand out from more professionally designed graphics. Examples of this type of visual content include handwritten notes on napkins or post-it notes. These can be quickly created and often generate more engagement than more polished graphics. This type of content can help to add authenticity to a brand.

GIPHY Branded GIFs

GIFs can be a useful way in B2B marketing to capture the attention of busy audiences who tend to skim through online content. It is an effective way to capture users' attention, add a touch of humour or fun to dull content, and communicate your marketing message in a time-efficient and engaging way.

GIFs can be viewed anytime, anywhere without requiring audio or a large file to be downloaded. Here are some tips for designing GIFs for your B2B marketing efforts:

- Use a short excerpt from an existing video to convey the main points of your message.
- Include GIFs in email marketing to increase click-through rates.
- Create educational GIFs by combining screenshots to show an idea, steps, or a process.
- Use GIFs to highlight product features.
- Design GIFs to address frequently asked questions or provide how-to information.

Occasionally use GIFs on social media to engage with users and facilitate conversations.

Using GIFs in your marketing communication can help to convey your brand message in an engaging and fun way, while being cost-effective and concise. You can utilise GIFs in email marketing and on social media to create a compelling brand image.

TOOLS FOR CREATING VISUALS

Canva

Canva is a user-friendly graphic design tool that allows you to easily create professional-looking visual content for your marketing and social media campaigns. It offers a wide variety of pre-designed templates, elements, and tools that make it simple for users to create visually appealing designs without the need for advanced graphic design skills.

Venngage

Infographics and fresh data are among the most-shared types of content on social media. Venngage is a graphic design platform with a focus on creating professional-quality infographics.

With its spreadsheet import feature and hundreds of customizable chart configurations, Venngage makes it easy to create visually striking infographics that effectively communicate complex data and ideas.

In addition to its infographics tools, Venngage also offers a wide range of built-in graphics and branding resources, allowing you to fully customise infographics to match your own branding and style.

Creatopy

Creatopy (formerly Bannersnack) is a graphic design tool that offers a range of features specifically tailored towards marketing. Some of these features include design sets and brand kits to help manage and organise branding materials, and the ability to easily edit designs for different formats (such as desktop or mobile) in a single click, which can save a lot of time. These features are particularly useful for agencies working with multiple clients or social media accounts.

Creatopy also offers a variety of design templates and resources, such as stock photos and graphics, to help users create professional-looking marketing materials quickly and easily. In addition, the platform's user-friendly interface and intuitive drag-and-drop editor make it easy for users to create custom designs from scratch.

Infogram

Infogram is a web-based platform that enables users to create interactive and visually appealing infographics, reports, and dashboards. It offers users a variety of customizable templates, elements, and tools to create professional-looking visual content without the need for advanced design skills. The platform also allows users to import data from various sources and offers the ability to download visualisations in different formats or embed them on websites. Additionally, it allows to track audience engagement through analytics, and update the dashboard with live data. With Infogram, businesses can effectively communicate complex information to their target audience in an easy-to-understand format.

Flaticon

Flaticon is a comprehensive online library of high-quality vector icons and graphics that can be used in a variety of design projects, including websites, presentations, social media posts, and more.

With Flaticon, you can easily search for the perfect icon or graphic to suit your needs, using a variety of filters such as style, colour, and category. The platform offers over 5 million icons and graphics in a wide range of styles and formats, including SVG, PNG, and Font.

In addition to providing a vast selection of icons and graphics, Flaticon also offers a range of features to help designers create professional-quality designs. These features include a user-friendly editor that allows users to customise the size, colour, and shape of icons, and the ability to download icons in bulk.

Jasper

If you are struggling to come up with visually appealing and on-brand images for your B2B blog posts, Jasper.ai's art feature can help.

Their AI-powered design tool allows you to easily create custom graphics and visual content for your blog without the need for expensive design software or graphic design skills. Simply input your brand guidelines and desired text or imagery, and Art will generate a variety of designs for you to choose from.

Not only does Art save you time and money on design resources, it also ensures that all of your visuals are consistent with your brand identity. This is especially important for B2B companies, as building trust and credibility is crucial for attracting and retaining business customers.

In addition to creating new visual content, Art can also optimise your existing graphics for different platforms and resolutions. This means you can easily repurpose your content for social media, email marketing, and other channels, saving you even more time and effort.

Free Image Resizer | Resize Your Images Online | Promo.com

Promo.com's Imagery Sizer is a tool that resizes images for various marketing materials, including social media posts and ads. It supports multiple file formats and platforms, such as Facebook, Instagram, and Twitter.

The tool automatically adjusts dimensions to fit the required size, and offers advanced features like text and graphic overlays, filters, and colour adjustments. Its versatility, ease of use, and advanced features make it a valuable tool for creating professional marketing materials.

VIDEOS

INTRODUCTION

Videos should be an important part of your B2B content strategy.

"95% B2B buyers say videos play crucial role in their purchase decisions"[24]

Spiceworks

Video is an essential component of modern media consumption habits and is a powerful marketing tool for B2B brands. With over one billion hours of YouTube content being watched daily, it's clear that a significant portion of B2B audiences is consuming video content. In fact, 80% of internet traffic is video content and 87% of marketers use video in their strategies.

The success of video marketing can be attributed to its ability to engage and inform viewers in a concise and visually appealing way. It can be easily shared on a variety of platforms, including social media, and can add a personal touch to B2B interactions.

By creating informative and engaging brand videos, B2B companies can enhance their brand awareness, increase social engagement, build consumer trust and loyalty, and reach and convert prospects.

Additionally, video marketing can help B2B companies stand out in their industry and outperform competitors in terms of organic reach.

Many businesses limit the use of online videos to the final stages of the sales process such as product demonstrations, but leading companies are utilising them throughout the entire sales funnel and different marketing channels to meet the increasing demand for video content from customers.

---

[24] https://www.spiceworks.com/marketing/content-marketing/news/b2b-buyers-say-videos-play-crucial-role/

> **TIP:** Even though video production can be costly and challenging, investing in genuine, practical and relevant videos can have a significant impact without breaking the bank.

TYPES OF VIDEOS FOR B2B

Vlogs, or Video Blogs

Vlogs can be an effective B2B marketing tactic for these reasons. First, vlogs allow you to showcase your products or services in a more engaging and visual way. While text-based content is important for providing information and details, vlogs allow you to demonstrate your products or services in a more dynamic and interactive way. This can be especially useful for complex or technical products that may be difficult to explain through text alone.

In addition, vlogs can help you establish the company's brand personality and create a more human connection with the audience. By featuring real people within the company, vlogs can help humanise the brand and make it feel more approachable and relatable. This can be especially useful for B2B companies, which may be perceived as more formal or impersonal.

Vlogs can also be an effective way to drive traffic and engagement on your company's website or social media channels. By creating engaging and informative vlogs, you can attract new visitors and encourage them to share the content with their own networks, increasing the reach and visibility of the company's message.

Product Videos

Use your products as inspiration for the topics of your product videos. These demos and instructional videos are designed to showcase a specific product or service and demonstrate to B2B audiences how they can use it. This helps to increase brand awareness and allows viewers to understand the benefits of the product. When presented by an influencer or brand ambassador, product reviews and demonstrations are even more impactful to audiences. Unboxing videos, where an influencer reveals and reacts to a new product, are particularly popular and can keep viewers engaged.

- Viewers are anywhere from <u>64-85% more likely to buy after watching a product video</u>[25].
- <u>73% more visitors</u>[26] who watch product videos will make a purchase.
- Product videos help explain products better and answer users' questions.
- Video viewers also stay longer on site.

You just can't go wrong with product videos. So, if you can afford them, use them.

Explainer Videos

Explainer videos are designed to educate and inform viewers. Brands can use these videos to promote their company, answer questions, and discuss products and services, as well as to announce upcoming promotions, webinars, and other events. B2B marketers often use explainer videos to introduce their product or service to viewers, increasing brand awareness and generating leads.

Tutorial Videos

Tutorial videos provide viewers with step-by-step instructions on how to do something, along with helpful tips. The topic of the tutorial is up to the brand, if it is relevant to the audience and has a clear connection to the brand's product, service, or mission

Video Interviews

B2B buyers may not have the opportunity to meet with the CEO or interact with industry experts in person, but they can watch videos featuring these individuals. Video interviews allow B2B brands to

---

[25] https://www.linkedin.com/pulse/those-who-view-product-videos-6485-percent-more-likely-chris-o-mary/
[26] https://animoto.com/blog/business/small-business-video-infographic/

showcase important figures within the company or bring in expert guests and influencers. This helps to foster conversation between the brand and its audience, build trust, and establish the brand as a valuable source of engaging and relevant content.

Influencer Marketing Videos

Influencer videos showcase industry thought leaders and experts that your viewers will be familiar with and excited to watch. These videos can take many forms, such as interviews, tutorials, or Q&As, if the topic is relevant to the audience. It's important when making an offer to an influencer, ensure it is attractive (e.g., new exciting ideas) and make it easy for them to film the content.

Event Coverage Videos

Event coverage videos are meant to provide viewers with a glimpse of industry and brand events, whether they were online or physical. They may include footage of the location and activities, as well as interviews with attendees, speakers, and organisers.

Testimonials and Case Study Videos

B2B consumers tend to trust other buyers and their experiences with brands, so it can be an effective strategy for B2B companies to showcase their best success stories in a compelling and easy-to-understand video format

User-generated Content Videos

Video strategies don't always have to involve creating new content from scratch. Sometimes, curating existing content can be effective as well. Depending on the industry, user generated content may be a viable option for some B2B brands, particularly if customers or users are actively sharing videos related to the brand's products, services, or events.

Animated Videos

Animated videos featuring cartoons or graphics can also be a useful component of a B2B content strategy. These types of videos are particularly effective for explaining complex ideas or technical products and services in a visually appealing and light-hearted manner.

Time-lapse Videos

Time lapse videos are created by taking a series of photos over a set period and compiling them into fast-moving footage - this is a function on smartphones. B2B brands can use time lapse videos to document live events, for example. Time lapse videos are visually appealing, for example to show large crowds in events, or booth activity.

Shorts or Short-Form Videos

Without a doubt, one major shift in platform usage that will quickly differentiate brands will be the adoption of short-form video. This shift towards short-form video can be attributed to the widespread popularity and success of TikTok, which has led to it becoming the preferred content format for many consumers.

Attention spans may indeed be getting shorter, but I believe this is not the only reason why shorts are gaining popularity. The reality is, there is still a demand for long-form content such as videos, blogs, and podcasts. However, people are consuming content more frequently, everywhere, and in shorter bursts due to its accessibility in various situations and settings throughout the day. This has led to a shift in the way content is being created to fit into the constantly changing background of people's lives.

After TikTok, other social media networks have also launched their own short-form video features, including YouTube: YouTube shorts were introduced in September 2020. It was initially tested in India, where it became an instant hit. It was then released globally and has seen over 6.5 billion daily views. YouTube Shorts offers new creative tools, such as a multi-segment camera and the option to add music from a large library, and it is easy for viewers to discover new content as it has its own row on the home page and can be easily swiped through on mobile devices.

Short-form videos are typically 15 to 18 seconds long. B2B Brands should consider including Shorts in their marketing strategy. Brands can start with YouTube, as it allows them to tap into YouTube's massive mobile user base and maintain a presence on the platform as more users adopt the feature. It is a simple and effective way to share short, engaging videos to other platforms

TOOLS FOR CREATING VIDEOS

Vimeo

Vimeo is a well-known video software solution that offers a variety of features for professionals, teams, and organisations. With Vimeo, users can create branded videos, host webinars, onboard employees, host virtual town halls, monetize video content, and more.

The platform also includes marketing tools such as customer acquisition and engagement tools, analytics dashboards, licensed stock videos, team collaboration, marketing asset libraries, and user-friendly interfaces. It also has security features such as Single Sign-On access and SCIM.

PEECH

Peech is a platform that assists marketing teams in creating, transcribing, optimising, and publishing videos. The company was founded by Danielle Dafni, who has experience in media marketing, video editing, visual design, and media art.

Danielle understood the challenges that marketers and content creators often face when trying to convert written content into videos without having the necessary video creation skills. The platform uses AI technology that allows marketers, content managers and social media managers to produce professional videos using their own media without having to hire external video services, saving on costs.

OFFEO

Offeo is a cloud-based online design platform that enables users to create professional-quality designs for a variety of purposes, such as social media posts, marketing materials, and branded content. With Offeo, users can access a wide range of customizable templates, graphics, and design elements to create visually appealing designs quickly and easily.

In addition to its design capabilities, Offeo also offers a range of features for collaboration, project management, and team communication, making it a useful tool for businesses and teams working on design projects. Some of the key features of Offeo include:

- Easy-to-use drag-and-drop editor
- Wide selection of customizable templates and design elements
- Collaboration and project management tools
- Automatic saving and version control
- Export options for various file types
- Integration with popular design and productivity apps

Truvid

Truvid is a technology-based platform that delivers exceptional video experiences for publishers and viewers. They have developed a business model that connects publishers, content creators and advertisers to a live video ecosystem, enabling them to communicate and interact with their audiences globally.

Truvid's innovative approach expands the reach of publishers and content creators and allows advertisers to target their ads to the right audience, by enabling all parties through this model, Truvid can offer unmatched video experiences that are advantageous to all involved.

Powtoon

Powtoon is a well-known video and visual communication platform that assists individuals, teams, and companies to achieve their objectives by transforming communication into visual experiences that catch attention and motivate action from their target audience. Initially developed to help marketers and business owners to get attention, today the platform has grown to become a multi-purpose tool that can be used in various settings such as business presentations, product introductions, digital and broadcast advertisements, and explanatory videos.

Runway

RunwayML is a platform that offers a wide range of AI-powered tools to help users with their creative projects. These tools allow users to generate new ideas, create and edit content in new and innovative ways. The platform has a wide variety of tools available, such as image and video generation, text generation, and style transfer, to name a few. Furthermore, RunwayML is constantly updating and adding new tools every week, which means users will always have access to the latest and most advanced AI technology. With these tools, users can push the boundaries of what's possible and create truly unique and original content.

Free online video editor - Crop, filter, trim, and more

Magisto is an AI-powered video creation with video marketing templates and tools. The company's platform is powered by Vimeo and utilises artificial intelligence to analyse videos, identify areas for further optimization, and edit the video for maximum impact.

Marketers can also use Magisto to embed videos across channels, track analytics, and store videos in a secure, cloud-based location.

Soapbox - A Free Webcam and Screen Recorder for Chrome

Soapbox is a simple to use platform that enables users to produce high-quality videos with minimal equipment and effort. By using the Chrome extension and a webcam, users can record and edit videos featuring their webcam, screen, or a split-screen view.

This simplifies the video creation process and allows marketing teams to quickly build a library of engaging and informative content by merging talking-head recordings with screencasts and presentation materials.

Additionally, users can easily share their videos with their target audience or create a gallery on their website through Wistia Channels to drive traffic.

Panzoid

Panzoid is a free, customizable way to create an impressive YouTube intro for your channel. While there may be a bit of a learning curve at first, this powerful tool offers a wide range of features and resources for creating professional-quality videos.

Synthesia

Turn any text into a video with a fake human using an easy way to create engaging video content for your B2B marketing campaigns is with Synthesia.io.

Their AI-powered video creation platform allows you to easily turn text, images, and other static content into high-quality, professional-looking videos. Simply input your desired content and select from a range of customizable templates and styles, and Synthesia.io will generate a video for you in minutes.

Not only does Synthesia.io save you time and resources on video production, it also allows you to create a consistent visual brand identity across all of your marketing materials. This is especially important for B2B companies, which rely on building trust and credibility with their customers.

In addition to creating new video content, Synthesia.io also offers tools for video optimization and distribution, helping you reach a wider audience and get more value out of your video marketing efforts.

Pexels

Pexels is a free stock video platform that provides high-quality, royalty-free videos for personal and commercial use. With a wide selection of videos in a variety of categories, including business, travel, food, and more, Pexels makes it easy to find the perfect video for any project.

In addition to offering a wide selection of videos, Pexels also makes it easy to search for and download the videos you need. You can search for videos by keyword, colour, or duration, and you can easily download videos in a range of resolutions to suit your needs.

Renderforest

Renderforest is a cloud-based video and animation platform that offers a wide range of tools and resources for creating professional-quality multimedia content.

With Renderforest, users can create everything from promotional videos and explainer animations to logo reveals and music visualisations. The platform offers a variety of templates and assets to help users get started, as well as advanced features like green screen support, custom animation, and real-time collaboration.

In addition to its video and animation tools, Renderforest also offers a range of marketing and branding resources, including logo makers, business card generators, and social media post templates.

Renderforest is a comprehensive and user-friendly platform that can help businesses of all sizes to create engaging and effective multimedia content.

Wave.video

Wave.video is a video editing and marketing platform that allows users to create, edit, and share professional-quality videos for a variety of purposes, including social media marketing, content marketing, and video advertising. With an intuitive drag-and-drop interface and a wide range of customizable templates and assets, Wave.video makes it easy for businesses of all sizes to create visually striking and effective video content. In addition to its video editing tools, Wave.video also offers a range of marketing and analytics features to help users track the performance of their videos and optimise their campaigns. Wave.video is a powerful and user-friendly platform that can help businesses to streamline their video marketing efforts and engage with their audience more effectively.

Wistia

Wistia is a video marketing platform that helps businesses create and host videos, customise and track their performance, and improve engagement with their target audience. It provides a range of tools for recording, editing, hosting, collaboration, reporting, and management, as well as the ability to add call-to-action buttons and email capture forms to videos.

Wistia also offers integration with various CRM, analytics, marketing automation, sales, customer support, email, and compliance solutions. In addition to these features, Wistia also provides tools for video creation and collaboration, such as the ability to add annotations and captions, and the option to invite team members to review and provide feedback on videos.

With Wistia, you can gate your videos by requiring users to enter their email address to watch the video. Alternatively, you can place the email gate in the middle of the video and offer users the option to sign up to be notified of new content. By gating your videos in this way, you can collect email addresses from interested users and use this information to nurture and convert them into customers.

Pictory

Pictory is a tool that converts written content, such as blog posts, into videos. It allows users to select a blog post and have it transformed into a visual format, using a combination of text, images, and other media.

To use Pictory, users simply need to provide the URL of the blog post they want to convert into a video. The tool then uses natural language processing and other techniques to analyse the content of the post and generate a script for the video. Users can customise the video by adding their own images or media, as well as selecting from a range of formatting and styling options.

Once the video is created, users can publish it on their website or social media channels or share it with others through email or other means. By converting blog posts into videos, users can reach a wider audience and provide an alternative format for consuming content.

Pictory allows users to repurpose their blog posts and other written material in a visual format that can be more engaging and attention-grabbing for viewers.

PART FOUR:

CLIMBING THE SEARCH ENGINE RANKINGS

SEARCH ENGINE OPTIMISATION

INTRODUCTION

B2B search engine optimization (SEO) is a marketing strategy that B2B companies use to improve their ranking on search engines, particularly Google.

> "B2B SEO is an ongoing process of building trust and authority with your target audience. By creating and optimising valuable content, you can attract and convert more qualified leads for your business."[27]
>
> Brian Dean
>
> Founder of Backlinko

B2B SEO is an organic growth strategy, which makes it appealing for B2B companies who want to avoid relying on paid ads or pay-per-click (PPC). Unlike B2C SEO, B2B SEO often involves low search volumes and a more targeted audience.

It also takes time before your SEO efforts bear fruit, from 6 months to a year.

Technically, SEO works the same way for both B2B and B2C companies. Google's algorithms do not change based on the intended audience of the website.

However, there are some key differences between B2B and B2C SEO strategies. The main difference is that the target audiences for B2B and B2C companies are different, with different search intents and needs.

In B2B SEO, the target audience is typically a small group of decision makers with specific needs, whereas in B2C SEO the audience is more general and may be browsing for leisure. As a result, the strategies used for B2B, and B2C SEO should differ.

---

[27] https://backlinko.com/almost-done/seo-this-year-definitive-guide

STEPS TO BUILD SEO SUCCESS IN B2B

Here are steps recommended by Brian Dean, one of the world's most sought-after SEO experts.

Step One:

Research Your Buyers (See Part One of this Book)

The first step in creating a B2B SEO strategy is to conduct customer interviews or surveys.

To effectively reach B2B decision makers, it is important to create content that addresses their specific needs and concerns.

This can help your company stand out in a crowded field and ensure that your content resonates with your target audience.

Additionally, gathering information through customer interviews or surveys can help you understand the way B2B decision makers are using your product and inform the creation of content that targets different stages of the marketing funnel. Once you have this information, the next step in the strategy is to identify keywords for the bottom of the marketing funnel.

Step Two:

Identify your BOFU (Bottom of the Funnel) Keywords

At this point in the B2B SEO process, you should already have a list of bottom-of-the-funnel (BOFU) keywords, which are terms that potential customers use when they are ready to make a purchase.

These are important to focus on because they are closely related to your product or service and can lead to sales. It is important to include BOFU keywords in your B2B SEO strategy, but it is also important to have a holistic approach and target keywords from all parts of the marketing funnel. Starting with BOFU keywords can ensure that you have the most important, sales-driven keywords in place.

> **TIP:** To find unique and specific bottom-of-the-funnel keywords for your B2B business, you can use your customers' words and phrases as keywords, use tools like GrowKeywords to generate long-tail keywords, or reverse engineer your competitors' keywords by using an SEO tool like Ahrefs or SEMRush.

It is also important to not focus solely on high-volume keywords, as low-volume keywords with high competition from competitors can also be valuable.

Search volume tools may not always be accurate, so it is important to consider other factors such as competitor interest when evaluating the potential value of a keyword. Most internet searches are long and specific, so focusing on these "long-tail" keywords can be a good way to find valuable, low-volume keywords.

> **TIP:** If you find a keyword that is relevant to your product or service and has a high cost-per-click (CPC), it would be wise to target that keyword, even if it has low search volume. Filter out any keywords that have a CPC of <$1.00 (or $5.00 if you sell a high-ticket item) to filter out junk keywords that will not convert for you.

There are many tools available to search for keywords, as outlined under tools in this section.

Step Three:
Identify Top of the Funnel (TOFU) Topics

The next step is to identify a set of high-level keywords and topics, which will be the basis for creating blog content. These are known as "top of the funnel" keywords, and they have a higher search volume compared to "bottom of the funnel" terms. By focusing only on the bottom of the funnel keywords, you are limiting the potential traffic from Google.

Top of the funnel refers to the marketing activities carried out to create awareness about a brand or product. It is part of the theoretical customer journey also called a "purchase journey."

TOFU helps marketers spread awareness, educate prospects, and create a buzz about a product, service, or brand.

The long-term value of SEO comes from targeting top of the funnel searches, as at any given time, only a small percentage of leads are ready to buy, while the majority are still in the research phase. By targeting these high-level keywords, you can turn these visitors into customers over time. Instead of trying to make a sale immediately, the focus should be on capturing their contact information and adding them to an email list. Then, by providing valuable content and positioning yourself as an expert in your field, when they are ready to make a purchase, your brand will be top of mind.

Step Four:

Enhance Product and Service Pages for SEO

In this step, you will optimise your product and service pages for SEO by focusing on one of the specific, low-level keywords identified in Step #2 on each page.

> **TIP:** Create Original Content. It is essential that each landing page has entirely original content. Failure to do so may result in duplicate content issues, which will negatively impact search engine rankings.
>
> Make it long. Short landing pages tend to have a hard time ranking in search engines because there is not enough information for Google to fully comprehend the page. It should be at least 500, to 2000 words.
>
> Use the right Keywords. It is essential to include your target keyword multiple times on your landing page (do not overuse it though!). Mention the keyword in the H1 title and title tag, ensure that the page URL includes the target keyword, using synonyms and variations of the main keyword, create a unique meta description and place the keyword high up on the page within the first 50 words.

Step Five:

Create a high-value B2B Blog

Blogging is a crucial aspect of a legitimate B2B SEO strategy. This is because a valuable blog can improve SEO in a variety of ways. For instance, publishing high-quality content can attract links which in turn can help your landing pages rank better in search engine results.

Additionally, a B2B blog can establish you and your company as a reliable source of information in your industry, which according to a report by The Content Marketing Institute, can help build trust with your target audience.

> **TIP:** A common mistake made by many B2B companies is to write blog posts that focus solely on their products or services. Don't do it!
>
> Instead, it's recommended to write about related topics, known as "shoulder topics," that are not directly linked to your product or service. Ultimate guides are an effective option for those new to B2B content marketing, as they tend to perform well. Finally, it is essential to avoid using a boring and stiff writing style in B2B content. A more approachable and professional "Business Casual" writing style is recommended.

Step Six:

Obtain Backlinks for Your B2B Website

Link building is crucial for achieving success with B2B SEO. The challenge is to obtain quality backlinks for your B2B business, particularly if you are in a "dull" industry. Some strategies specifically designed for B2B include:

1. Digital PR, focusing on industry blogs and news sites instead of mainstream media.
2. Creating helpful tools and calculators that are easy to use and share.
3. Utilising partner pages from suppliers, manufacturers, or other strategic partners you do business with and asking to be added to

their list of companies they work with.

INNOVATIVE TACTICS TO CLIMB THE SEARCH ENGINE RANKINGS

Avoid Cannibalization

If you have multiple pages on your website that are competing to rank for the same keyword, it is important to consolidate them to avoid keyword cannibalization.

This occurs when Google is unsure which of your pages to rank for a particular keyword, potentially leading to your competitors outranking you. To fix this issue, redirect any competing pages to the one that most closely addresses the search intent using a 301 redirect, and consider re-optimizing or rewriting the content if necessary.

Consolidating pages in this way can be a quick win for your B2B SEO strategy and can help improve your rankings.

Build Topical Relevance

B2B companies often invest in content that is not directly related to their products, such as glossaries, because it can help build topical relevance for their websites. Google tends to rank websites that are topically relevant at the site level, rather than individual pages, so it is important for B2B companies to regularly produce well-written and well-optimised content on a particular topic to rank well.

This can be more effective than simply focusing on product-related content, which may be less interesting to readers and may not help to increase traffic or build the brand.

> **TIP:** By producing a high volume of high-quality content on a particular topic, B2B companies can become more relevant in their industry and may be able to outrank competitors with higher domain authority.

Consider Search Intent

It is important to consider more than just search volume and cost-per-click (CPC) when selecting keywords for your B2B SEO strategy. Search intent, or the purpose behind a user's search, is also a critical factor to consider.

Research and understand the meaning and intent behind the keywords you are targeting in your B2B SEO strategy. Otherwise, you may find that a keyword you thought was relevant to your business has a different meaning or connotation, leading to confusion or a lack of success in ranking for it. To avoid this, make sure to fully understand the intent behind all the keywords you choose to target.

Use Topic Clusters

As you create content to build topical relevance for your B2B website, it is important to organise it into topic clusters or content silos.

This involves grouping related content together and breaking down broad topics into more specific subtopics. All the child pages in a topic cluster should link back to the main "pillar page," which is the main page for the topic cluster. In some cases, this may be a feature page for your product or service. Organising content in this way can help improve the visibility and relevance of your website to search engines.

Creating a large volume of content that covers the main subject of your topic cluster can help you:

- Connect with users who have very specific search intent
- Address all aspects of the topic
- Rank well for broader keywords
- Dominate search engine results pages (SERPs) for related keywords
- Build up your topic cluster through internal linking, which is the process of linking to other pages within your own website. This is an important step in your B2B SEO strategy.

Maximise Internal Linking

Internal linking, or the process of linking to other pages within your own website, is just as important as external linking in a successful B2B SEO strategy.

Internal links help visitors and search engines navigate your website and understand its structure and hierarchy. While external backlinks are important, they should not be prioritised over internal linking. A systematic approach to internal linking, such as keeping a spreadsheet of your content organised by category and adding links to related content with every new piece, can help improve the effectiveness of your topic clusters and topical relevance efforts. It is also a good idea to periodically add links to new content in older posts.

External Link Building with data-rich Content

As discussed in Step Six above, link building, or the process of acquiring external links to your website, is an important aspect of a successful B2B SEO strategy. It can be a challenging and time-consuming task, but it is necessary to improve your visibility and rankings in search engines. While there are unethical or "black hat" link building practices to avoid, it is still necessary to engage in "white hat" link building, which involves building genuine, high-quality links.

One effective way to do this is to create data-rich content that other websites may want to reference or link back to, such as statistics or proprietary studies. While this type of content may not directly convert into sales, it can still drive valuable links to your website.

The Skyscraper Technique for External Link Building

The skyscraper technique [28] is a content marketing strategy that involves creating high-quality, in-depth content on a specific topic, and then promoting that content to attract links and increase visibility in search engines. This technique was first popularised by Brian Dean, the founder of Backlinko, and has become a popular approach for B2B marketing.

There are several key steps involved in implementing the skyscraper technique:

1. Research: Identify a specific topic or keyword that is relevant to

---

[28] https://backlinko.com/skyscraper-technique

your business and has a high search volume.

2. Content creation: Create a comprehensive, well-researched piece of content on the chosen topic that goes above and beyond what is already available on the web. This could be a blog post, white paper, or other type of content.

3. Promotion: Once your content is published, promote it through social media, email marketing, and other channels to attract links and drive traffic to your site.

4. Link building: Use outreach techniques to convince other websites to link back to your content, which can help increase its visibility and improve its search engine rankings.

By following these steps, you can use the skyscraper technique to create high-quality content that stands out in their industry and attracts links, traffic, and leads.

> **TIP:** An untapped SEO Strategy from Brian Dean is creating your own keyword. Your brand is already a keyword that you automatically rank for, but you can also rank for keywords that you create. An example for this is the Skyscraper Technique, which is a term Brian coined and now receives over 2000 searches per month, with most of them leading to a specific website. To do this you can give a concept a new name or add a twist to something that already exists. This can be seen with terms such as Inbound Marketing, Chatbots, Influencer Marketing, which were all concepts that existed for a long time before someone gave them a name and made them popular. When you give something a name, it becomes real and becomes yours!

Link Building with Search Ads

Link building with search ads involves promoting link-worthy content, such as statistics and original research, expert quotes, and infographics, through paid search ads.

This approach is based on the concept of the "vicious circle of SEO," which states that people search for something, read the top result, and some of them link to that content, leading to the page remaining at the top of the search results.

By paying for exposure at the top of the search engine results page (SERP), businesses can potentially acquire new backlinks.

The main benefits of this approach include the possibility of lower costs compared to manual outreach efforts and mostly passive participation. Additionally, some of the traffic generated by the search ads may result in other actions, such as trial signups and newsletter subscriptions, which can further increase the return on investment (ROI) of the campaign.

One challenge of link building with search ads is attribution, as only a portion of the acquired backlinks will be directly attributed to the search campaign.

Capture Voice Search with Long Tail Keywords

With the increasing use of virtual assistants like Amazon's Alexa and Google Assistant, more and more people are using voice search to find information online. As a result, it's important to consider how voice search may affect your SEO strategy.

One key aspect to consider is the use of long tail keywords. Voice search queries tend to be more conversational and natural, often in the form of a question. As a result, long tail keywords, which are longer, more specific phrases, may be more effective in attracting voice search traffic.

For example, rather than using the keyword "integration software," a long tail keyword might be "What is the leading provider of integration software?" This more closely matches the way a person might ask a question using voice search.

By incorporating long tail keywords into your search strategy, you can increase the chances that your website will rank for voice search queries and attract more qualified traffic. It's also a good idea to optimise for featured snippets, as these are often used to answer voice search queries.

The rise of voice search emphasises the importance of creating content that is natural, informative, and easy to read for both humans and search engines.

Prune your Content

Content pruning is the practice of removing low-quality content - often referred to as Zombie Pages - from your website in order to improve your overall SEO performance. This works because domain authority is distributed among all the content on your website.

By removing weak or low-quality pages, the remaining pages on your website will receive more of the authority and rank higher in search results. It's important to get rid of weak content because it dilutes the overall strength of your website.

> **TIP:** You can use a decision tree, like the one provided by HubSpot, to help determine which content on your website is performing poorly and should be pruned.

Optimise Your Existing Feature and Services Pages

Once you have identified your bottom-of-the-funnel B2B keywords, it is important to optimise your existing feature and services pages for these keywords before creating new content. If you do not have a separate page for each feature, it is a good idea to create one.

Each feature or service should have its own page, optimised for its own keyword, and these pages should be linked to both in the menu and footer of your website.

As you create additional or new content, make sure to link back to these feature pages to improve their ranking for the targeted keywords and demonstrate their relevance. This is an important part of your "foundational SEO" strategy.

Google Snippets to Organically Rank on Top Quickly

Using snippets, also known as featured snippets or position zero, is a technique that can help your website rank highly in search engine results pages (SERPs). A snippet is a summary of an answer to a search query that appears at the top of the SERP, above all other results. It is meant to provide a quick and concise answer to the user's question, and it can often be pulled from a webpage or other source on the internet.

For B2B companies, ranking highly in search results can be especially important, as many of their potential customers may be actively searching for information related to their products or services. By optimising your website for snippets, you can increase the chances that your content will be featured in this prominent position, which can lead to increased traffic and potential sales.

To optimise for snippets, it is important to understand what types of questions users are asking and how your content can provide valuable and relevant answers. You should also ensure that your content is well-organised and easy to read, as snippets are typically brief and to-the-point. Additionally, you can use structured data and other technical SEO techniques to improve the chances that your content will be eligible for inclusion in snippets.

By following these steps, you can increase your chances of ranking highly in search results and attracting more visitors to your B2B website.

Move Subdomains to Subcategories

It may be more beneficial for SEO to move a blog from a subdomain (e.g., blog.website.com) to a subdirectory (e.g., website.com/blog) because doing so may help to avoid confusion for search engines and prevent the dilution of backlink strength due to the separation of keywords under a subdomain.

However, using subdomains can still be useful in certain circumstances, such as when each subdomain functions as a separate entity within a larger corporation and the backlinks to each subdomain do not dilute the topical focus of the site. An easy-to-understand example of this would be Disney, which has multiple subdomains that serve different purposes, such as cars.disney.com, videos.disney.com, and princess.disney.com.

Purchase Existing Domains That Are Expired

To improve your website's search engine optimization (SEO) efforts, you can consider purchasing existing domains that are related to your niche and redirecting it to your current domain.

This can help your website inherit any links and anchor text that the previous domain had, which can improve your domain authority and increase traffic from SEO.

However, it is important to ensure that the new domain has a good topical trust flow, un-optimized anchor text, and was not previously used for spam. Go to GoDaddy's Expired Domain Auction.

Get on Top of X List

To drive targeted traffic to your site, consider finding a popular "top x" list related to your business and paying the author to include you on the list. This type of content tends to attract high-intent readers who are actively seeking recommendations or solutions, so if the page receives a significant amount of traffic, the investment in being included on the list is likely to quickly pay off in terms of increased visibility and potential conversions.

TOOLS FOR SEO

"Be prepared for SEO success without paying a thing!"[29]

Shailesh Panchal

There are many sophisticated and free tools out there that can ensure your website pages upload super-fast and your site is free of any technical errors, is keyword optimised and is secure.

It takes the assistance of technology to analyse data, conduct research, validate code, and perform other SEO site audit checks at a large scale.

These tools are super helpful in identifying and addressing issues related to content, keywords, and website structure, ultimately improving search engine rankings and user experience.

The long list of free tools is categorised into:

- Content-Related Tools
- SEO Website Crawlers
- Mobile SEO
- Website Technical Audit

---

[29] https://shaileshpanchal.com/

- Website Security Audit
- Website Performance
- Others

Content-Related SEO Tools

SEODataViz

One free tool that may be useful is the SEO Ngram Tool, developed by Ryan Jones, Vice President of SEO at Razorfish. This tool helps you understand common keyword combinations and generates a search term relationship map, grouping different search terms into a visual map that shows the base keyword terms (primary connections) and the search terms related to them.

AnswerThePublic

Free Keyword Generator Tool: Find 100+ Keyword Ideas in Seconds

Keyword Generator by Semrush

These tools have been mentioned under buyer research as well.

Ahrefs or SEMRush offers a variety of free SEO tools, including the Free Keyword Research Tool, which provides top keywords with associated volume for different search engines like Amazon, YouTube, Bing, and Google.

Ahrefs and SEMRush sources this data from the Google Keyword Planner, clickstream data, and data partnerships. This tool can be useful for generating article writing topics.

Competitor Keyword Analysis is a method where you use an SEO tool to obtain a list of keywords that a competitor's website is already ranking for in search engine results pages (SERPs). This approach is efficient because it quickly provides many keywords. For example, by using SEMrush on a competitor's website, one can get a list of over 212k keywords.

Seed Keywords

Seed Keywords is a powerful tool that helps businesses and marketers identify the right keywords to target in their SEO and PPC campaigns. The platform is designed to make keyword research quick and easy, allowing users to find relevant and profitable seed keywords in a matter of minutes. With Seed Keywords, users can easily uncover new keyword ideas and opportunities, as well as get valuable insights on search volume, CPC, competition, and more. The tool also offers a number of advanced features such as keyword grouping, filtering, and analysis, making it a versatile and comprehensive solution for businesses of all sizes and industries.

Google Autocomplete

Google Autocomplete is a useful strategy for discovering long-tail keywords. To use it, begin typing a term into the Google search bar and take note of the suggested autocomplete options.

Link Intersect by Ahrefs: Find More Backlink Opportunities

More on linking, one way to find backlink opportunities is to also use the Ahrefs Link Intersect tool. This tool allows you to see all the websites that are linking to your competitors, but not to your own website. If a website is linking to several of your competitors, there is a good chance that they will be open to linking to your website as well. By using the Link Intersect tool, you can identify potential opportunities to gain valuable backlinks that can help improve your search engine rankings and drive traffic to your website.

Siteliner

This is a free duplicate content scanner provided by CopyScape (an anti-plagiarism service). It is useful for identifying pages within a site that have similar content and spotting opportunities for improving content. It is best for articles to feature unique content, as having too much content that is similar can create a situation where Google may have to choose which page is more relevant and make one page canonical. The scanner is limited to 250 pages, but it can alert you to possible problems with thin pages.

The W3C Markup Validation Service

The validator also checks the heading outline (H1, H2, etc.) on a web page. This tool can be useful for understanding how Google sees your web page or a competitor's web page.

By ticking the "Show Outline" option, you can see how your heading elements appear to a search engine. The results may reveal issues with your website template. If the validator encounters bad HTML, you can try restarting the process and selecting a document type in the "More Options" section to get around the coding errors.

SEO Website Crawlers

Screaming Frog SEO Spider Website Crawler

This is a free website crawler that analyses up to 500 URLs. It is an industry-leading site auditing software that can identify issues such as broken links, duplicate content, and redirect chains. It also provides information on page titles, metadata, and header tags, as well as insights into website structure and performance.

SEOquake

SEO Qualie is the SEO Book Keyword Tool, which provides data on keyword popularity and competition.

Netpeak Software

Netpeak Spider is another crawling tool that has a generous free version that can crawl up to 100,000 URLs.

The tool provides data on over 80 SEO-related issues and checks on over 100 technical website issues. The free version of the Netpeak Spider makes a useful complement to the free version of Screaming Frog, as they both have different features and present data in different ways.

Find broken links on your site with Xenu's Link Sleuth (TM)

Xenu Link Sleuth is the old-school SEO tool of choice when it comes to a free site crawler.

It's described as a broken link checker, and it does a great job of that. It generates a report for both internal and external broken links.

But Xenu does so much more than check for broken links.

Xenu can output a report that provides a quick overview of page titles, orphaned pages, redirects, and pages that are not found (404 response codes).

Mobile SEO Tools

Mobile SEO is incredibly important. That's why it's essential to be able to test what a search engine results page (SERP) looks like in virtually any city in the world.

It's also useful to be able to check what your web page looks like in the most popular mobile phones. Pages that look great tend to convert better.

MobileMoxie

Page-oscope: Preview Websites on Various Phones

SERPerator: Free SERP Checker & Mobile Keyword Rank Checker

MobileMoxie provides a fully functional Mobile SEO Tools.

The MobileMoxie SERP checker shows you what the rankings look like in a huge selection of mobile phone screens.

What makes this tool especially helpful is that it can be localised to any city in the world.

Thus, you can test what the mobile rankings are for someone located in any city in the world. This is great for local SEO or for client work where you're not located in the client's area.

There is also a MobileMoxie Web Page Checker that can show you what your web page looks like in virtually any mobile phone. This will help you optimise your web page so that it converts the best across a wide range of mobile phones. The tool is fully functional and can be used for free three times.

You can also scroll through the local SERPs (Search Engine Results Page) for any city in the world in virtually any language of your choosing.

Website Technical Audit Tools

DNS Checker

The DNS Checker tool will check how well your site is revolving around the world. This tool can help surface issues with the server settings that can affect the ability of Google and other site visitors from reaching a website.

This tool can be used to identify why Google's crawler could not reach a website, causing massive indexing issues. The cause was a bad server setting.

So, if search engines or users are having difficulty reaching the website, give the DNS Checker tool a try.

Email Blacklist Check - IP Blacklist Check - See if your server is blacklisted

This online tool will check if your domain or IP address is on one of several popular blacklists. Being on a blacklist can affect email deliverability.

Website Security Audit Tools

Many SEOs don't consider security as part of an SEO audit, but website security should be a component of an SEO audit.

A secure website is a major part of how well it ranks and encourages sales.

WPSec

This free vulnerability scanner offers a quick but comprehensive scan of potential issues.

Create the report, then research whether your site has issues that need fixing. WPScans.com is a useful tool for beginning a security audit.

SSL Server Test (Powered by Qualys SSL Labs)

The SSL Labs Security tool will spot misconfigurations and security holes in your HTTPS certificate implementation.

Adding a server security certificate is touted as being easy, but that's not always the case. This useful tool will help you diagnose hidden issues.

Hacker Target Drupal Security Scanner

Drupal Security Scanner | HackerTarget.com

This free and comprehensive security scanner will highlight common issues with a Drupal-based website.

Website Performance Tools

GZip Compression Checker

The GZip Compression tool checks if your site is using GZip compression. Using compression allows your server to download your web pages quickly.

YSlow

The free YSlow Performance Audit tool is a comprehensive performance audit scanner. It creates a report of 23 performance rules.

GTmetrix

GTmetrix Speed and Performance Audit is another tool that will generate various benchmark scores. Use these scores to understand where your site can be improved.

TIP: Do not forget Google Analytics, which offers a range of great features for tracking website traffic and performance.

Google of course offers many SEO-related tools.

PageSpeed Insights

Rich Results Test - Google Search Console

Lighthouse for Google Chrome

Aside from the Google Search Console, which is very important and is worth mentioning, here are other useful tools provided by Google for auditing and inspecting web pages and websites: Page Speed Insights offers web page speed feedback.

Rich Results and Structured Data Testing Tool has been consolidated with the Rich Results tool. This helps diagnose issues with your structured data and confirms whether the structured data qualifies for rich results.

The structured data validator does not verify if your structured data conforms with Google's guidelines.

Make sure you are following Google's Structured Data Guidelines. Making a mistake with structured data could result in a manual penalty.

Google Lighthouse is a tool that's built into Chrome. It is also available as a Chrome Lighthouse Extension.

Google's Lighthouse is an incredible suite of web performance analytical tools.

The Lighthouse SEO report focuses on how well the site can be indexed, which is an especially useful feature these days. Lighthouse can be used to diagnose on-page issues related to the code and to help find out what's making a site slower plus it offers tips on how to improve those shortcomings.

Lighthouse is a must-learn tool for everyone who wishes to improve their site performance metrics.

Others

Ranked AI

Ranked.Ai offers SEO tools and services to help small and medium-sized businesses and agencies scale their online presence. Its platform includes a range of features designed to make SEO easier and more effective, including tools for blog content creation, link building, and optimization.

One of the main benefits of using Ranked.Ai is that it helps businesses and agencies improve their search engine rankings, which can lead to more traffic and higher visibility online. By optimising their website and content for relevant keywords and phrases, users can increase the chances of their website appearing at the top of search results, which can help them attract more visitors and potential customers.

In addition to its SEO tools, Ranked.Ai also provides support and guidance to help users get the most out of its platform.

Mozbar Browser Extension for SEO

Mozbar is a browser extension that allows users to analyse the SEO and social media performance of websites. It is designed to help users understand how websites rank in search engines and identify areas for improvement.

Once installed, Mozbar appears as a toolbar in the user's browser and can be used to analyse any website they visit. It provides a range of data and metrics related to SEO and social media, including the website's Domain Authority (a measure of the overall strength of a domain), the number of inbound links and social shares, and the presence of key SEO elements such as title tags and meta descriptions.

Mozbar also includes a range of features to help users optimise their own websites, including a keyword research tool, a page optimization tool, and a link building tool. These tools allow users to identify opportunities to improve their website's visibility in search engines and to track the success of their optimization efforts.

SEARCH ENGINE MARKETING

INTRODUCTION

Search engine marketing (SEM) or pay-per-click (PPC) is a strategy used to increase a company's visibility that appears on search engine results pages (SERPs) through paid advertising. This approach differs from search engine optimization (SEO), which focuses on improving organic search rankings, as SEM allows companies to pay for their content to appear higher in search results with a "sponsored" or "ad" label.

SEMis a highly effective and efficient way to quickly generate leads from the internet. It allows for precise targeting, including geographic location, demographic, and language group, making it more cost-effective than traditional forms of advertising like radio or television.

Many businesses are using SEM to increase their market share. However, if not executed correctly, SEM can become costly and produce no return on investment.

> **"Search engine marketing is the most efficient way to reach B2B buyers. It allows you to target your ideal customer at the moment they're searching for a solution."[30]**
>
> Michael Brenner
>
> CEO of Marketing Insider Group

If you refer to the top trends in B2B Marketing, most B2B buying processes begin with an online search. In fact, the average B2B buyer conducts 12 different online searches before interacting with a website.

This certainly highlights the importance of search in B2B marketing. While SEO can be effective, it requires a significant amount of time. On the other hand, SEM can be activated immediately, and can yield 50% more conversions than organic advertising.

With the right digital marketing strategies, PPC campaigns can drive lead generation and sales. Google Ads specifically allows businesses to target

---

[30] https://marketinginsidergroup.com/author/mbrenner/

their audience at all stages of the buying process and present them with tailored messaging where 90% of B2B researchers are already searching for information.

STEPS FOR SEM SUCCESS

Step One:

Embrace the B2B sales cycle. In SEM, it is important that you are embracing the B2B sales cycle: Recognizing that the B2B sales cycle can take an average of 3-4 months and using that time to build a trusting relationship with customers through PPC. Tailor your Google Ads content, offer, and copy to fit the mindset of a decision-maker at the stage they're in.

Step Two:

Stay organised. Additionally, you need to stay organised. Understanding the structure of Google Ads, making one account per website, and creating campaigns and ad groups that are organised by purpose. Many B2B Google Ad professionals choose to organise groups by funnel stage.

Step Three:

Research keywords extensively. Understanding the business and industry is crucial for successful B2B Google Ads, and research needs to be as specific as possible. Knowing exactly what search terms your target audience is typing into Google search is essential. (Read More under PART FOUR: SEO Strategies)

Keywords can be grouped into four main categories: generic, branded, competitor, and related, and it's important to cover all four categories when researching keywords.

Setting up a brainstorm with your sales team is also useful as they can provide insight on the specific pain points your target audience is facing and what they may be searching for.

Step Four:

Target Audiences. Utilise tools to identify businesses that have visited your website and add the user domain of the IP addresses as a custom audience within your Google Ads. Exclude IP addresses coming from your competitors to save on ad spend.

Step Five:

Consider Negative Keywords. Utilising a negative keyword list helps prevent wasting ad spend. Negative keywords can be related to job seekers, and other words not related to your product or service such as intern, career, resume, employer and part-time, full-time, hiring.

Step Six:

Use the SKAGs (Single Keyword Ad Groups) Approach. The SKAG approach is a way to structure your Google Ads account to achieve higher performance and maintain control of your account. By creating ad groups with only one keyword in them, you can make sure that the keywords you're bidding on match the search terms you're paying for, thus avoiding "The Iceberg Effect" and sinking like the Titanic.[31]

Step Seven:

Optimise the ad copy. To optimise an ad copy, it's best practice to speak to pain points, personalise copy to the CRM stage, be specific and use numbers when possible, keep it simple, stand out from the competition, use social proof, and use extensions. (Please read Part Two: Craft Killer Content, where a section is dedicated to ad copies)

Step Eight:

Optimise the landing page. To optimise landing pages, it's best practice to ditch the top navigation, have a clear call-to-action, keep it relevant to the ad, have strong copy, include hero image and visuals, and communicate the benefits and features of the product or service.

---

[31] https://www.linkedin.com/pulse/iceberg-effect-ppc-how-sink-like-titanic-igor-babic

Step Nine:

Measure and optimise continuously. PPC campaigns require ongoing attention to fine-tune details such as headlines, landing pages, and offers. This can be achieved through A/B testing and monitoring metrics. Connecting Google Analytics to Google Ads will provide more information on campaign performance. Managing PPC campaigns can be time-consuming, but there are tips available to maximise the value of time spent

Step Ten:

Run retargeting campaigns. Retargeting is an effective way to stay in contact with website visitors. Referring to Category Targeting, 95% of visitors will not be ready to purchase yet. Google Ads has a feature called Remarketing Lists for Search Ads (RSLAs) which allows retargeting lost conversions. An RLSA campaign can result in a significant reduction in cost per acquisition.

INNOVATIVE TACTICS IN SEM

Bid on Your Competitors Keywords

Bidding on your competitors' brand terms can be an effective way to improve the performance of your online advertising efforts. If someone is searching for your competitors' products or services, it's likely that they may also be interested in what you have to offer.

By bidding on these terms, you can capture the attention of this audience and potentially convert them into customers. It's important to ensure that you are doing this in a way that is legal and follows best practices for online advertising.

Additionally, by targeting specifically to keywords related to issues or problems with your competitor's products, you can get in front of an audience that may be interested in considering alternative options.

For example, you could bid on keywords such as [competitor's name] + help/support/contact, which suggest that users are experiencing difficulties with their product.

On top of bidding on your competitor's brand keywords, you can also create content that ranks for these keywords. This can be an effective way to capture the attention of users who are at the decision stage and may be considering multiple options.

Examples of content that could be effective in this context include comparisons of your product and your competitor's, lists of pros and cons, pricing information, and reviews.

By creating this type of content, you can provide valuable information to users who are actively considering your competitor's product and help them make an informed decision.

Remarket to Your Competitors' Web Visitors

Running a remarketing campaign to the visitors of your competitor websites can be a highly effective way to reach a targeted audience and drive traffic to your own website.

Remarketing campaigns allow you to show targeted ads to users who have previously visited your website or engaged with your brand online. By targeting the visitors of your competitor websites, you can reach a highly relevant audience who may already be interested in your products or services.

To set up a remarketing campaign to the visitors of your competitor websites, you will need to use a marketing platform that offers this feature, such as Google Ads. First, you will need to create a list of your competitor websites and then create a custom audience in your marketing platform that includes users who have visited these websites.

Next, you will need to create your remarketing ads and select your custom audience as the target for your campaign. You can then set your campaign budget, schedule, and other parameters to control how your ads are shown to your target audience.

By running a remarketing campaign to the visitors of your competitor websites, you can effectively reach a highly relevant audience and drive traffic to your own website. This can help you increase brand awareness, generate leads, and boost sales for your business.

Google: Geo Rollout Strategy

When launching a new product, consider a geo-rollout strategy where you roll out the product on all ad platforms in one location or area at a time, rather than spreading your ad budget thin across multiple locations. This can help create the impression that your company is larger and more established, while also being a more efficient way to allocate your ad budget. By focusing your efforts in one location at a time, you can ensure that your ads are seen frequently and create a strong presence in that area.

Combine Dynamic Search Ads (DSA) and Retargeting Lists for Search Ads (RSLA)

To expand the reach of your advertising while minimising risk, consider creating a Google Search campaign that combines Dynamic Search Ads (DSA) and Retargeting Lists for Search Ads (RSLA). This will allow you to target past website visitors only, broadening your reach while keeping it relatively low risk.

Exclude your Account Keywords from Your DSA (Google Dynamic Search Ads).

To avoid the negative impact of cannibalization on your campaigns' cost-per-click (CPC), it's recommended to exclude keywords used in other campaigns when implementing Google Dynamic Search Ads (DSAs) - a strategy discussed under the "Avoid Cannibalization" section of SEO Tactics

Retargeting: Targeting Users with Personalized Ads Using Enriched Data

One way to create highly targeted ads is to use Clearbit Reveal to retarget users based on enriched data, such as their company industry, tech stack, job role, or seniority.

By segmenting your audience in this way, you can create more personalised and relevant ads that are more likely to resonate with your target audience.

Clearbit Reveal allows you to gather insights about your website visitors and use this information to create targeted retargeting campaigns that are tailored to the specific interests and needs of different groups of users. This can help you reach the right people with your ads and increase the chances that they will engage with your content or take the desired action.

TOOLS FOR SEARCH ENGINE MARKETING

SEMrush

SEMrush is a powerful digital marketing tool that provides in-depth insights and data on advertising performance across various platforms.

It offers a suite of features specifically designed to help businesses improve their paid advertising campaigns, including keyword research, competitor analysis, and ad copy optimization.

The tool provides detailed information on search engine marketing (SEM), display advertising, social media advertising and video advertising. It also allows businesses to track competitors' advertising strategies, making it easier to stay ahead of the competition.

WordStream

WordStream is a digital marketing software that specialises in providing tools and insights for managing pay-per-click (PPC) advertising campaigns. The platform offers a variety of features including keyword research, ad group and campaign management, and performance tracking.

It also includes a set of tools for optimising ad copy, landing pages and conversion rates. WordStream is great to improve the ROI of their PPC campaigns. The software is designed to make it easy to manage and optimise large-scale PPC campaigns, making it a popular choice among digital marketers and advertisers.

Supermetrics

Supermetrics is a marketing data analytics and reporting software that automates the process of collecting, integrating, and analysing data from various sources. It helps companies to connect and retrieve data from platforms such as Google Analytics, Google Ads, Facebook Ads, Bing Ads, and more.

Supermetrics also allows users to create custom reports and dashboards to visualise the data, which can be shared with team members and stakeholders.

This tool is mainly used for marketing and advertising data analysis, and is a popular choice among digital marketers who need to make data-driven decisions.

Optmyzr

Optmyzr is a pay-per-click (PPC) management software that provides a range of tools to improve and automate their PPC campaigns.

The platform offers a variety of features including keyword research, ad group and campaign management, and performance tracking. It also includes a set of tools for optimising ad copy, landing pages and conversion rates.

Additionally, Optmyzr provides a set of PPC audit and optimization tools which enable businesses to quickly identify areas for improvement and make data-driven decisions. The software can be integrated with Google Ads and Microsoft Advertising, which allows businesses to manage their PPC campaigns more efficiently. Optmyzr is a great solution to improve the ROI of PPC campaigns.

SpyFu

SpyFu provides businesses with data and insights on competitors' search engine optimization (SEO) and pay-per-click (PPC) advertising strategies.

The platform offers a wide range of features, including keyword research, competitor analysis, and ad copy optimization.

It also offers tools to track and analyse competitors' backlinks and organic search visibility. This information can be used to improve your own SEO and PPC strategies and stay ahead of the competition.

SpyFu offers a wealth of data and insights, including historical data, which can be used to identify patterns and trends in your competitors' campaigns.

SE Ranking

SE Ranking is a comprehensive digital marketing tool that provides businesses with a wide range of features for managing and optimising their search engine optimization (SEO), pay-per-click (PPC) advertising, and social media campaigns. The platform offers a variety of tools for keyword research, competitor analysis, and website audit, among other features. It also includes a set of tools for monitoring and analysing website traffic, as well as for tracking and managing backlinks.

PART FIVE:
UNLEASHING THE POWER OF SOCIAL MEDIA

INTRODUCTION

According to Global WebIndex research, 59% of the world's population uses social media[32], with an average daily usage of 2 hours and 29 minutes as of July 2022. Social media networks continue to be popular among various demographics and are constantly evolving. And social networks have transformed marketing, including in B2B.

> **"Today, 40% of B2B buyers use social media to help inform their purchasing decisions."[33]**
>
> Gartner

More and more B2B buyers are using social media to inform their purchasing decisions, with 40% of B2B buyers utilising social media in this way. As a result, B2B marketing leaders are allocating an average of 12.2% of their marketing budgets towards social media, as reported by Gartner[34].

Social media is also a powerful tool for software marketers looking to expand their product's visibility and generate leads. However, with so many B2B social media platforms to choose from, it can be difficult to determine which ones to focus on. To assist software marketers, this chapter lists the four key B2B social media platforms to invest time and resources in: LinkedIn, YouTube, Facebook and Twitter.

---

[32] https://www.smartinsights.com/social-media-marketing/social-media-strategy/new-global-social-media-research/
[33] https://www.gartner.com/en/digital-markets/insights/b2b-social-media-channels-for-software-marketers
[34] https://www.gartner.com/en/digital-markets/insights/b2b-social-media-channels-for-software-marketers

KEEP THIS IN MIND

Social Media for Lead Generation

While LinkedIn and other social media are important for audience growth and brand building, they are often not enough on their own to generate leads and sales.

According to a survey by the Content Marketing Institute, Social media is the top distribution method for B2B content marketers, with 89% using social tools.[35]

However, while social media is effective for brand awareness, building trust and credibility and educating the market, very few reported that social media was an effective channel for driving direct leads and sales.

To convert followers into paying customers businesses should proactively engage their audience and steer them towards their products or services. With the time and resources invested in social media, B2B Marketers should always be a means of identifying and nurturing sales prospects.

This involves reaching out and connecting with followers, rather than simply waiting for them to come to you.

Ensure to put calls-to-action (CTAs) on every piece of content you publish in social channels and link the posts to a website or landing page.

Here are **Three Social Media Content Ideas that Convert:**

Targeted Content

Basing your content from your buyer persona research, build highly targeted content that would trigger readers to respond or engage.

---

[35] https://contentmarketinginstitute.com/articles/b2b-industry-benchmarks-budgets-trends-research/

"Hand-Raiser" Content

Hand Raiser content is useful to identify people in your audience who have expressed interest in your offerings or have problems that your offerings solve

Content that Sparks Discussion

Using the research in the early section of this book, build relevant content that sparks discussion and reach out to start a helpful and meaningful conversation with customers.

INNOVATIVE TACTICS TO SUCCEED IN SOCIAL MEDIA

Monitor Competitors

Keep an eye on what your competitors are doing on social media to get an idea of what strategies are effective and see if you can borrow any ideas for your own campaigns.

Benchmarks keep evolving so it is good to see the growth and engagement rates of your competitors.

Always Create Original, Useful Content

Avoid simply curating content from other sources and instead focus on creating original, creative content that will engage your audience.

Think about ways you can make your followers' (work) lives easier or more enjoyable. Provide content and resources that delight them in some way.

Thought leadership is particularly important, as highlighted in this book.

Drive Employee Advocacy

It's essential for companies to stand out and connect with prospects on a deeper level. One effective way to do this is through employee advocacy on social media.

Employee advocacy is the practice of encouraging and enabling employees to share company-approved content on their personal social media channels. This can include blog posts, infographics, videos, and other types of content that are relevant to the company's industry and target audience.

One of the key benefits of employee advocacy is that it allows companies to showcase their expertise and thought leadership in a more authentic and personal way. Rather than simply promoting products or services, employees can share their own experiences and insights, which can help to build trust and credibility with prospects.

In addition to providing high-quality content for employees to share, companies can also make it easy for them to do so by giving them access to sharing tools and platforms like Oktopost. This platform offers a range of features specifically designed for driving employee advocacy, including an employee advocacy platform, a content library, and social media scheduling and publishing capabilities.

> **TIP:** To encourage employee participation in advocacy efforts, companies can consider offering incentives and rewards. This could include a kick-off competition with a substantial prize, such as a trip to a global conference or visit to headquarters for an event. Ongoing monthly incentives can also be a good way to keep employees engaged and motivated.

Take Advantage of New Features & Formats

A strategy for increasing the reach and engagement of your social media posts is to take advantage of new features as they are introduced by the platform. For example, when Facebook introduces a new feature like Facebook Live or LinkedIn introduces a feature like embedded slides, these features may receive a temporary boost in reach to encourage adoption.

To take advantage of this, be sure to test out and use these new features in your posts. This can help increase the reach and engagement of your content and give you a leg up over competitors who are not leveraging the new features. It is important to stay up to date on the latest features and innovations offered by social media platforms and be proactive in testing and incorporating them into your social media strategy.

Maintain a Consistent Brand Voice

Ensure that your social media presence consistently reflects your brand identity and messaging.

Enable Customer Support

Monitor and respond to customer support issues in a timely manner to improve customer relationships and show that you are there to help on every channel.

Experiment

Try out different types of posts and posting times to identify what works best for your audience.

Be Engaging

Interact with your audience and encourage them to engage with your content.

Run Contests

People love a good contest! Contests can be a useful marketing tactic for B2B businesses to achieve various goals, such as increasing followers on social media, gathering customer testimonials, boosting exposure, or gathering product feedback.

To run a successful contest, it's important to first define your goals and then outline the parameters, including the audience, budget, prize, staff and resources, time limit, type of contest, and judging criteria.

Promotion is key to the success of a contest, and there are several options to consider, such as sending a dedicated email, adding it to your company newsletter, sharing in blog posts, leveraging social media.

A social media contest could involve asking followers to share a photo or video related to a particular theme or topic, or to use a specific hashtag when posting about the business. This could be an effective way to drive engagement and increase followers on social media platforms.

1. **Video contest:** A video contest could involve asking participants to create and submit a video related to a particular theme or topic, such as showcasing how they use your product or service. This could be an effective way to generate user-generated content and showcase the value of your products or services.

2. **Product feedback contest:** A product feedback contest could involve asking customers to provide feedback on a particular product or service and rewarding the most useful or creative feedback with a prize. This could be a useful way to gather valuable insights and improve your products or services.

3. **Blog writing contest:** A blog writing contest could involve asking participants to write a blog post related to a particular theme or topic and rewarding the best submissions with a prize. This could be an effective way to generate fresh content and showcase the expertise of your business.

THE FOUR KEY B2B SOCIAL MEDIA PLATFORMS

LinkedIn: Leading the Pack in B2B

LinkedIn is the number one platform for social media B2B marketing. According to a report by the company, 89% of B2B marketers use LinkedIn for social media B2B lead generation[36].

As a leading platform for professional networking and lead generation, LinkedIn has over 830 million members[37] and is one of the most trusted and efficient platforms for B2B software marketers, with 40% of B2B marketers stating that it is the best tool for generating high-quality leads. A survey by the Content Marketing Institute found that LinkedIn was the most effective social media platform for B2B lead generation, with a conversion rate of 2.74%[38].

LinkedIn is ideal for reaching high-level decision-makers and offers various targeting options such as job title, job function, company name, company size, and location. According to LinkedIn, out of all its users, 180 million[39] are senior-level influencers. That makes up nearly 25 percent of its total user base. At 63 million, more than one in eight LinkedIn users are decision-makers and about 10 million are categorised as C-level executives.

The content that works best on LinkedIn is typically informative and provides valuable business insights, for example, how a product or service can improve an organisation's operational efficiency. To enhance your LinkedIn strategy, it may be useful to consider utilising best practices.

---

[36] https://www.linkedin.com/pulse/linkedin-better-than-any-other-social-platform-b2b-lead-kumkum-katha/
[37] https://kinsta.com/blog/linkedin-statistics/
[38] https://www.linkedin.com/pulse/what-best-social-media-b2b-lead-generation-facebook-linkedin-vickers/
[39] https://business.linkedin.com/marketing-solutions/ad-targeting

In the near future, LinkedIn will become increasingly prevalent.

LinkedIn is expected to see an increase in the number of creators and influencers, particularly due to the departure of brands and businesses from Twitter.

To accommodate this influx of users, LinkedIn is introducing features like Twitter, such as the option to control who can comment on your posts. Additionally, there seems to be a growing emphasis on SEO on the platform.

To be successful on LinkedIn, sales and marketing professionals should be aware that people are fed up with generic and boring LinkedIn messages and dull content and strive to create more authentic and engaging content that resonates with their audience.

> **TIP:** B2B buyers not only expect personalised attention, but also expect brands to set high standards. To meet these expectations, it is important for companies to focus on posting valuable, engaging content rather than superficial material, and to make use of LinkedIn Events and LinkedIn Live to engage with their communities in real time.

LinkedIn will continue to prioritise engagement by rewarding accounts that actively participate in conversations, with company pages and individual profiles that leave meaningful comments on relevant posts being particularly successful on the platform. Brands that take a creative approach to their LinkedIn content will be well-positioned to succeed.

Finally, people don't want to be sold to want their problems solved by people who they believe care. As per the authenticity trend, this will resonate more than ever, especially on LinkedIn.

> **TIP: Optimising LinkedIn Posts**
>
> To optimise your LinkedIn posts, keep them concise (ideally between 150 and 1,200 characters):
>
> - For videos, aim for a length of 30-90 seconds.
>
> - Posts with images tend to perform better than those without, so consider including still images.
>
> - While it can be effective to incorporate personal content into your marketing strategy, be sure not to overdo it and try to tie it back to the professional context.
>
> - It is believed that a greater focus on personal content can lead to a decrease in overly sales-focused content, as people recognize the importance of building relationships in business and converting leads.

INNOVATIVE TACTICS FOR LINKEDIN ADS

Use LinkedIn Ads to Distribute Quality Content for Free

When you make your content freely available without requiring visitors to leave their contact information, buyers are more likely to consume as much of it as possible without worrying about being spammed.

When they are ready to make a purchase, they may look you up on Google and request a discovery call.

While both gated and ungated content can be effective, test out ungated quality content as well.

Use LinkedIn Sponsored Messaging

Sponsored messaging on LinkedIn can be more effective than traditional LinkedIn ads.

These ads, called Message Ads, stand out in a less crowded environment, and deliver a targeted message with a single call-to-action button, making it easier to drive engagement and increase response rates.

The ads can lead prospects to a Lead Gen Form for easy lead collection, and provide reporting that allows you to track who is engaging with the ad.

Additionally, Conversation Ads offer a more engaging experience, allowing you to deliver multiple offers and types of content within a single message.

These ads can drive prospects to multiple landing pages or Lead Gen Forms and provide insights on how many people interact with the content and offers, as well as how engaged they are in the conversation.

Experiment with the New LinkedIn Retargeting Feature

LinkedIn Ads has been introducing new features at a rapid pace, which is exciting for advertisers. However, the costs of advertising on the platform have also been increasing, presenting a challenge for marketers.

On the positive side, this trend suggests that more marketers are finding value in LinkedIn Ads and are willing to increase their budgets and spending. It is also likely that some marketers are using the default bidding method (maximum delivery), which allows LinkedIn to bid aggressively for impressions and drives up competition.

Recently, LinkedIn Ads has introduced several effective retargeting methods, including the ability to target users who have interacted with a single image sponsored content ad, watched at least 25% of a video ad, or visited a company page. Experiment with these new features.

Look out for LinkedIn Future Releases

LinkedIn is releasing several new features soon that every B2B Marketer should be aware of.

One of these features is the ability to promote personal profile posts, which is a departure from the current ability to only promote company page posts. This will likely be beneficial for companies whose executives frequently share high-quality content on the platform.

Another new feature is the ability to use "click to message" ads, which will allow for more natural and unscripted conversations and relationship building compared to the current "conversation ads" that use pre-scripted messages and calls to action.

Additionally, LinkedIn will release a revenue attribution report that helps advertisers better understand the impact of their campaigns on the sales cycle, particularly for B2B advertisers who often face challenges in tracking the effectiveness of their efforts over long periods of time and through multiple decision makers.

Facebook

Facebook is the largest social media platform, with a user base of almost 3 billion[40].

Many advertisers believe that it is only useful for B2C companies and that B2B companies should avoid using it for advertising, but it is a misconception.

Facebook ads, if executed the right way, can be very profitable for B2B companies, as they can drive website traffic, leads, and sales.

85% of B2B Marketers[41] who use social media remain dedicated to Facebook. It allows businesses to empathise with prospects and connect with them on a more personal level, by utilising its features and targeting capabilities such as lead capture forms, custom audiences, lookalike audiences, and dynamic ads to reach and engage their target audiences.

Facebook is great for those looking to build stronger relationships with prospects and customers, and B2B marketers can target users by location, interest, demographic and behaviour to reach the right prospects at the right time.

> **TIP:** Keep in mind that content that is easy to understand and ready to consume works well on Facebook. Boost the B2B marketing results on Facebook by sharing case studies, how-to guides, videos, using hashtags; targeting a specific audience and posting regularly with consistent messages.

---

[40] https://sg.oberlo.com/statistics/how-many-users-does-facebook-have
[41] https://komarketing.com/industry-news/85-of-b2b-marketers-who-use-social-media-remain-dedicated-to-facebook-4486/

Six Tactics for Facebook Ad Success

1. The key is to **focus on targeting the right person with the most relevant message at the right time** by considering the audience's position in the buying journey. This will help determine the message and ad type that will have the most impact.

2. **Provide clear and relevant value** through your ads, as Facebook prioritises ad content based on its relevance to the audience. It assigns a score between 1-10, based on the expected number of positive or negative interactions the ad will receive, and this score can serve as a benchmark for the ad's performance. Use lead magnets like eBooks, downloadable research reports, webinars to incentivize buyers to engage and provide their contact information.

3. Additionally, **choose the right ad format and placement**, such as image, video, or carousel. The choice of ad placement, such as the news feed or right column, can also affect the reach and cost of the ad. It's important to consider the competition and audience engagement while making a choice.

4. **Optimise Facebook ads for mobile** users to maximise reach and engagement. Facebook puts a lot of emphasis on helping advertisers reach mobile users and most of its growth comes from mobile ads.

> **TIP:** To optimise ad campaigns for mobile are keeping ad copy short, ensuring that videos can be viewed without sound, and making sure the landing page is mobile-friendly. In general, the same rules that apply for desktop ads also apply for mobile ads.

5. **Exchange Pixel Data for Facebook Ads**. To reach new audiences on Facebook through advertising, you can consider sharing your pixel data with other advertisers. By exchanging data with companies that have similar audiences but are not direct competitors, you can potentially expand the reach of your ads and reach new users. This strategy can be an effective way to target a larger audience without significantly increasing your ad budget.

6. **Overcome Ad Blockers.** If a high percentage of your target audience uses ad blockers, especially on Facebook, consider using a static image pixel instead of a JavaScript pixel. Ad blockers may not

block static image pixels, which could help ensure that your ads are still visible to your target audience. This strategy can be particularly effective if your target audience includes millennial gamers or mobile users, who may be more likely to use ad blockers.

Twitter

With over 450 million monthly active users[42], Twitter allows real-time conversations. B2B businesses can use it as part of their social media marketing strategy to connect with prospects and turn them into customers.

B2B marketers can use Twitter to reach a large audience in real time, engage in relevant conversations, and offer practical insights. Effective content on Twitter includes real-time insights, advice, or news updates, such as live conference updates to position oneself as a thought leader in the industry.

Twitter is not typically a top choice for B2B companies in terms of marketing efforts, often ranking behind Facebook, Google and LinkedIn.

Twitter's ad platform is also less advanced than Facebook or Google, with limited conversion tracking, lack of effectiveness for direct response marketing and a lack of engaging, value-communicating ads. Twitter does, however, offer targeting options such as interest targeting, behaviour targeting, and lookalike audiences to help marketers reach their target audience.

B2B companies can invest a small amount and reach potential customers via the platform.

There is also less competition on Twitter compared to Facebook and Google.

> **TIP:** Twitter ads can be a hidden gem for B2B marketers because it allows you to target a specific audience that follows certain micro-influencers in your company's industry. This is something that cannot be done on other social media platforms.

The best practices for running ads on Twitter include amplifying well-

---

[42] https://thesocialshepherd.com/blog/twitter-statistics

crafted tweets that are already performing well organically, targeting followers of hidden gem accounts (great influencers from the Twitter community that are off the beaten path) and focusing on link click-through rates and engagement rates.

YouTube

YouTube is a video-hosting and streaming platform. As of 2023, YouTube is the second biggest social media in the world, with over 2.5 billion active users[43]. Only Facebook (2.9 billion) has more active users than YouTube. There are 4.65 billion active social media users worldwide. This means that 54.34% of active social media users in the world access YouTube.

B2B marketers can use YouTube to connect with their target audience, establish trust and generate leads by creating informative videos.

When using YouTube for B2B software marketing, it is important to consider that since video content appeals to everyone, YouTube can be used by people of all ages, backgrounds, and locations, making it a great channel for all types of B2B marketers.

YouTube also offers various targeting options such as location, age, gender, interests, and behaviour. Educational videos that address target audience's queries perform best on YouTube as people go to this platform for learning purposes.

> **TIP:** When creating videos for YouTube, it is important to keep them helpful, informative, and engaging.

The Rise of YouTube Ads

Advertising on Google and YouTube together can be very powerful and is likely to demand a larger share of ad budgets soon. There are several reasons why YouTube ads are on the rise.

One reason is that YouTube is popular among all age groups, with 62%

---

[43] https://www.demandsage.com/youtube-stats/

of users accessing the platform daily[44] (including myself!).

Additionally, YouTube and Google ads have been less affected by recent privacy updates like iOS 14.5, which has impacted the ability of other platforms to accurately track conversions.

Finally, the use of "Performance MAX" (PMAX) campaigns can drive YouTube views and conversions. PMAX allows advertisers to use seven ad channels (Search, Shopping, Display, Discovery, Gmail, YouTube, and Maps), including YouTube, in a single campaign and uses data from all channels to target new customers.

Note: I wouldn't necessarily recommend PMAX for B2B lead generation, especially for a bottom of the funnel offer like a demo or quote request. PMAX typically works best for B2C or ecommerce companies.

5 Steps for a Successful B2B YouTube Strategy

Step One:

Optimise Your YouTube Channel. YouTube is not just about the videos you post; your channel page is also an important element. It serves as your profile page on the site, it's where viewers will learn more about your brand and your company. Thus, it's vital to establish your channel page with comprehensive information, keep it consistent with your branding strategy.

When setting up your YouTube channel consider the following:

- Use your brand logo for your channel's picture, unless it's a personal brand, in which case use a headshot that's easily recognizable and memorable.

- Add a custom banner on the top of the page.

- Write a detailed description in the "About" field, make sure it's easily understood what your brand and channel are all about. It's also the perfect place to add a call to action or link to your website.

- Organise your video content into dedicated playlists that will be displayed on your channel page, this helps viewers find what they're looking for easily.

---

[44] https://www.globalmediainsight.com/blog/youtube-users-statistics/

- Optimise your channel for SEO by including industry keywords, YouTube is a prominent feature in Google searches, so an optimised channel can significantly increase your chances of ranking high in relevant searches.

> **TIP:** You can refer to Adobe Creative Cloud as an excellent example of profile optimization.

Step Two:

Plan and Implement Your Video Marketing Strategy. It's not enough to just post videos haphazardly, it's important to have a plan that aligns your marketing objectives with the needs of your target audience. Hold video brainstorming sessions to generate ideas that will appeal to your intended viewers.

Consider the following when developing your video marketing plan:

- Who is your target audience?
- What types of videos do you want to create?
- How are your competitors attracting audiences in your niche?
- How will you advertise and promote your channel?
- How much will you spend on promoting your videos?

Ensure consistency in your video marketing efforts by following a schedule.

According to social marketing expert Jeff Bullas, when his team lacked consistency, they were only getting 16 to 30 views per day. However, once they started posting 2 to 3 times a week, they gained over 1,000 views within a month[45], this highlights the importance of consistency in growing your channel.

---

[45] https://www.jeffbullas.com/youtube-channel-growth/

Step Three:

Optimise every video that is posted on the channel. This includes creating an attention-grabbing thumbnail, writing an engaging and unique title, writing a detailed video description with keywords and a call-to-action, and including relevant tags. By doing this, videos have a better chance of ranking high in search results on YouTube and Google. It is noted that IBM optimises all its videos for SEO, and it is recommended to do so as well.

Step Four:

Don't focus on your sales pitch. To effectively showcase your expertise and experience on YouTube, it's important to create content that demonstrates how you can help others and illustrates how your products and services can help solve their problems, rather than solely using videos as a sales pitch. Examples of successful video styles on YouTube include behind-the-scenes videos, product demonstrations, testimonials, and how-to videos. It's also mentioned that it's possible to create high-quality videos with equipment that you already own and some basic editing skills. However, for the best outcome it is recommended to invest in equipment like tripods, microphone to improve the production value of the content.

Step Five:

Analyse Your Data to Improve Your YouTube Strategy. To understand the impact of your videos on your viewers, it's important to track your analytics and understand where your strengths and weaknesses lie. This will allow you to identify trends and reactions, and better gauge how your target audience is interacting with your content.

The Most Significant YouTube Metric

When it comes to analytics, YouTube is distinct from other platforms. On social media, you're likely used to tracking metrics like likes, shares, followers, and retweets. On YouTube, you can still like and share content, but other metrics have a greater impact on your channel.

YouTube wants its users to like the content they see and engage with it, the most critical metric you'll see is your viewer retention. It is a measure of how long people who click on your videos watch them. YouTube values the quality of the content its users produce, and higher quality content that keeps viewers interested is more likely to rank high in search results.

To achieve the best viewer retention rate, it is necessary to create content that not only inspires people to click on it, but also encourages them to keep watching.

INNOVATIVE TACTICS FOR YOUTUBE

Bid on Competitor YouTube Videos

Use in-stream ads on YouTube to grab the attention of users watching videos about your competitors and potentially convert them into customers.

Google allows you to hyper-target your ads to specific videos, making it a valuable opportunity to capture the attention of your competitor's potential or existing users. There are two types of in-stream ads you can choose from: skippable ads, which allow viewers to skip the ad after 5 seconds but only charge you if the viewer watches at least 30 seconds of your video (or the full duration if it's shorter than 30 seconds) or interacts with your video; and non-skippable ads, which do not allow viewers to skip the ad but charge you for all impressions.

You can also use video discovery ads to reach users earlier in the process, by showing your banners on YouTube search results pages and driving users to your video when they click on the ad. By using these tactics, you can capture more real estate with your ads and increase the visibility of your brand on YouTube.

YouTube Pre-Roll Ads

One way to reach a targeted audience of your competitors' existing and potential clients is to use YouTube pre-roll ads. Pre-roll ads are short video ads that play before the main content on YouTube and can be an effective way to get in front of a high-quality audience at a relatively low cost. When creating your pre-roll ad, it's important to make the first 5 seconds engaging enough to avoid having your ad skipped.

This can help ensure that your ad gets the attention it deserves and has a better chance of being effective. By targeting your competitors' audiences with YouTube pre-roll ads, you can reach a relevant and engaged audience that may be interested in your products or services.

TOOLS FOR SOCIAL MEDIA

Oktopost

Oktopost is the only social media engagement SaaS designed by B2B marketers, for B2B marketers.

Oktopost is a social media management and employee advocacy platform that helps businesses manage their social media presence and drive employee engagement. It provides a range of tools and features for scheduling, publishing, and analysing social media content, as well as for creating and sharing content through employee advocacy. Some of the key features of Oktopost include:

- Social media scheduling: Oktopost allows users to schedule and publish social media content across multiple networks, including LinkedIn, Twitter, and Facebook.

- Employee advocacy: Oktopost includes tools for creating and sharing content through employee advocacy, including an employee advocacy platform and a content library.

- Social media analytics: Oktopost provides a range of analytics and reporting tools, including social media performance metrics and engagement analytics, to help users track the success of their social media campaigns.

- Social media listening: Oktopost includes a social media listening feature that allows users to monitor, and track mentions of their brand and industry keywords across social media platforms.

- Collaboration and workflow management: Oktopost includes tools for collaboration and workflow management, including the ability to assign tasks and track progress.

Oktopost is designed to help businesses manage and grow their social media presence, drive employee engagement, and measure the success of their social media efforts.

Hootsuite

Social media publishing and analytics tools are the second most popular technology used by B2B content marketers, with 81% reporting use of these tools.

The most common technology tool used by B2B content marketers is web analytics tools, with 88% reporting use. Hootsuite offers both types of tools. Hootsuite allows multiple team members to manage multiple accounts in one place and track customer queries, which can be assigned to the appropriate team member for a response.

The Hootsuite dashboard makes it easy to analyse social media performance, find the optimal times to post, and track the return on investment. Hootsuite's content library is also useful for B2B marketers, as it can be used to store pre-approved content and brand assets.

Brandwatch

Brandwatch tracks and analyses online conversations from over 95 million sources. It allows companies to monitor mentions of their brand, competitors, and customer sentiment, among other things. This analysis can be used to inform various business decisions, such as product development.

Social Media Customer Service - Sparkcentral by Hootsuite

B2B customers are typically high-value, and it is important to provide customer service options that meet their needs.

Sparkcentral is a tool that allows businesses to manage customer service through social media accounts, live chat, WhatsApp, and SMS. This allows companies to have full context and access to all customer interactions across all support channels, enabling them to quickly provide accurate and up-to-date responses to inquiries.

This level of customer service can help to improve customer satisfaction and increase the likelihood of them returning for future business, such as contract renewals or plan upgrades.

LinkedIn Hashtags Generator

Tucktools helps generate relevant hashtags for LinkedIn content based on topic and country. (Remember you can also use ChatGPT to recommend hashtags)

By entering a keyword or phrase related to your content, the tool generates a list of relevant hashtags that can be used to increase the reach and engagement of your posts on LinkedIn.

In the B2B context, hashtags can be a useful tool for driving content engagement by making it easier for users to discover and interact with your content. By using relevant hashtags in your LinkedIn posts, you can increase the visibility of your content to a wider audience of potential customers and partners. This can be especially helpful for B2B companies looking to reach other businesses and decision-makers on LinkedIn.

In addition to increasing the reach of your content, using hashtags can also help to build and engage your LinkedIn community. By participating in relevant hashtag conversations and using hashtags in your own posts, you can connect with other users and industry professionals who share similar interests and goals. This can help to establish your company as a thought leader in your industry and build relationships with potential customers and partners.

<u>Audiense</u>

Audiense is a social media tool that helps companies identify and segment their social media audiences.

This is useful for running targeted ad campaigns and understanding customer personas. The platform is focused on Twitter and is particularly useful for businesses seeking to understand more about their target audience.

Autoresponder Bots for Social Media

Autoresponder bots for social media are automated programs that are designed to respond to messages or comments on social media platforms. These bots can be used for a variety of purposes, such as answering frequently asked questions, providing customer support, or promoting products and services. They can be programmed to respond to specific keywords or phrases and can also be programmed to respond to messages in a specific language or region.

Some popular social media platforms that support autoresponder bots include Facebook, Twitter, and Instagram. The main advantage of using autoresponder bots is that they can save time and resources by automating repetitive tasks and allowing businesses to respond to customers quickly and efficiently.

However, it is important to note that while autoresponder bots can be useful tools, they should not be used as a replacement for human interactions, as they may not be able to provide the same level of personalization and empathy as a human customer service representative.

There are several examples like:

ManyChat: This is a popular bot platform that allows businesses to create chatbots for Facebook Messenger. It allows businesses to respond to customer messages, provide product information, and even handle e-commerce transactions.

Tars: Tars is an AI-powered chatbot builder that allows businesses to create chatbots for their website or Facebook Messenger. It can be used to answer customer questions, provide support, or promote products and services.

MobileMonkey: MobileMonkey is another popular bot platform that allows businesses to create chatbots for Facebook Messenger, WhatsApp, and SMS. It can be used for customer support, lead generation, and e-commerce.

Chatbot on Instagram: Instagram has also started to roll out the feature of chatbot on their platform, which allows businesses to provide customer support, answer frequently asked questions, and even direct users to their website.

Twitter bot : There are also some examples of Twitter bots that can automatically reply to tweets that contain certain keywords or hashtags. For example, a weather bot might automatically reply to tweets that mention the word "weather" with the current forecast for that location.

Social Blade

Spy on analytics on any profile on any social media with this tool.

PART SIX:

CONNECT WITH YOUR AUDIENCE AND DRIVE RESULTS WITH EMAIL MARKETING

INTRODUCTION

77% of B2B companies use an email marketing newsletter as part of their content marketing strategy and 79% of B2B marketers find email to be the most successful channel for content distribution.[46]

OptInMonster

Email marketing is not just for B2C businesses. B2B companies can also benefit from it.

Email marketing is the best way to increase loyalty, sales, awareness, and engagement metrics for B2B companies. It converts leads, and it is the most powerful channel for customer loyalty and retention.

59% of B2B marketers[47] consider email marketing to be their top channel for revenue generation.

However, some B2B brands don't understand how to use email marketing techniques effectively. This doesn't mean email marketing doesn't work, it means that you should take advantage of its effectiveness before your competitors catch up.

B2B EMAIL GUIDELINES BASED ON DATA

Best Time to Send B2B Emails

According to a report by SendInBlue, the optimal days for sending B2B emails are Tuesdays, Wednesdays, and Thursdays[48]. Wednesdays have the highest open rates. The best times to send these emails are between 12 am and 8 am, with 10 pm also resulting in high open rates.

---

[46] https://optinmonster.com/email-marketing-statistics/
[47] https://myemma.com/blog/9-sizzling-marketing-stats-from-this-summer/
[48] https://www.sendinblue.com/blog/best-time-to-send-email/

Email Frequency

To establish trust with B2B brands, it's important to follow through on your promises. If you commit to providing fresh weekly tips or monthly industry updates, make sure you fulfil those commitments. B2B email consistency is crucial. Stick to your schedule and avoid sending spam messages. B2B buyers are looking for valuable information that keeps them updated and informed. As for frequency, it is typical for B2B brands to send 1-3 emails per month[49].

GDPR

The General Data Protection Regulation (GDPR) is in place to protect customers by giving them control over their personal data. As a result, it requires businesses to obtain explicit consent from consumers before emailing them or using their data.

For B2B brands, GDPR requirements are less strict in that explicit consent is not always required before processing personal data to send B2B emails, if the sender is identified and contact information is provided within the email. This is considered sufficient for compliance purposes. It is different for B2C brands, where explicit consent is required before processing personal data and personal information cannot be obtained from buyers who don't provide active consent or want to keep receiving your emails.

For B2B brands, if there is a genuine reason, you can continue emailing business email addresses without active consent, as long as there is a legitimate interest, and you can justify the need to be contacting that address. The GDPR has stricter rules for B2C communication to protect individual buyers, but they cannot provide the same level of protection to B2B brands because B2B brands have other purposes for communication besides sales and marketing.

---

[49] https://coschedule.com/blog/email-marketing-sending-frequency

STEPS FOR B2B EMAIL MARKETING SUCCESS

Step One:

Define detailed buyer personas: Before developing a B2B email marketing strategy, create the various buyer personas. Determine which content would work for each persona. Do refer to Part One of this Book: Getting to Know your Dream Buyer.

Step Two:

Be strategic when cold emailing: Be strategic in your cold email approach for B2B email marketing. Avoid spamming your contacts, and instead, ensure your emails are valuable. Also, research who you're planning to email to personalise your communication wherever possible.

Step Three:

Use customer segmentation features: Use subscriber segmentation features that B2B email marketing platforms offer. As you progress your email marketing campaign, you'll find new ways to segment your subscribers.

Step Four:

Evaluate and choose the best B2B email marketing platforms: There are many email marketing platforms, so be sure about your choice. Evaluate the key features and pricing of B2B email marketing providers and decide based on what features and functions you need.

Step Five:

Create valuable lead magnets: Lead magnets are resources you offer leads in exchange for them to subscribe to your email list. You can use e-books, quizzes, guides, and whitepapers as lead magnets.

Step Six:

Optimise your email marketing campaign for mobile: Remember your mobile users when developing your email marketing campaign. Ensure your newsletters are mobile-optimised so users can always enjoy your emails.

Step Seven:

Pay attention to email design: B2B email design differs from B2C emails. Use A/B testing to determine how various templates and email structures perform. Do not underestimate the power of plain text emails. See tip!

Step Eight:

Leverage drip campaigns: Drip campaigns are automation solutions. When your target buyers interact with elements of your emails, this will trigger automatic responses.

Step Nine:

Track the vital data: Track and evaluate essential email marketing data to determine your campaign's success. Consider data like email open rates, bounce rates, subscribe and unsubscribe rates, and click-through rates (CTR).

> **TIP:** There is evidence to suggest that plain text emails can be more effective than HTML emails. According to a HubSpot study[50], HTML emails have a 23% lower open rate compared to plain text emails. Even plain text emails with just one image have lower open rates than those without images. Despite being visual creatures, people tend to prefer the personal feel of plain text emails as it is how we communicate with people we know. Not only do plain text emails have higher open rates, but they also have higher click-through rates compared to HTML emails which have 21% lower click-through rates. When planning your next campaign, consider testing the different formats, and identify the best choice for your audience.

INNOVATIVE TACTICS IN B2B EMAIL MARKETING

Personalise Your Subject Lines

Personalising subject lines is crucial for B2B campaigns, as open rates are generally only 15%[51]. This means that B2B companies need to take a more strategic approach when creating personalised email subject lines.

To develop engaging, targeted email subject lines for B2B email marketing, consider these tips:

Highlight your value proposition: Make it clear and obvious what you are offering, whether it be free high value content offers, or high-level tools.

Use a strong call-to-action (CTA): Use powerful CTAs like "watch this now", "you have to read this", and "sign up or miss out" in your subject

---

[50] https://blog.hubspot.com/marketing/plain-text-vs-html-emails-data
[51] https://clickback.com/blog/b2b-email-marketing-average-open-rates

line.

Speak like a human: Use conversational language that relates to your target buyers' pain points or desires.

Segment your audience: Your ideal buyers will differ, so segment your target audience into groups based on what they have in common and the personalised solutions you can offer. Use tailored subject lines when emailing different audience segments.

Keep it short: Research shows that subject lines 7 words or less perform 65% better[52] than those with 8 words or more.

Make Sure Your Content is Easy to Scan

When B2B buyers receive your email, it is important to structure the content in a way that is easy to scan. B2B emails should be brief as the recipient may not have the time to read a lot of text to understand your offer.

B2B buyers are likely to scan the content to quickly evaluate if the email is worth acting on. If the content is easily scannable and includes key points, it can convince the recipient to click through or at least read the email.

The goal of the email is to get the recipient to click through to your landing page or website to convert them and not for them to receive all the information in the email body.

To create easily scannable content for your B2B email marketing strategy, consider these tips:

---

[52] https://www.campaignmonitor.com/blog/email-marketing/best-email-subject-line-length/

Use short paragraphs and sentences: Keep text short and concise to make it easy to read.

Use bullet points: Bullet points make information easy to understand.

Use sub-headers: Sub-headers allow readers to quickly locate the points that matter to them.

Include images: Visual elements make emails more visually appealing and interactive.

Include external links for authority: Use external links to provide credibility and authority when mentioning statistics or data.

Send Milestone and Announcement Emails

It is important to send emails beyond just sales-driven newsletters. Customer loyalty is crucial for the success of a brand as new customers are only 20% likely to purchase, while existing customers have a 60 to 70% chance[53] of making a purchase.
B2B brands should include milestone and announcement emails as part of their communication strategy. They include:

- Welcome emails
- Anniversary announcements
- Sales target announcements
- New product launches
- New partnerships that affect your buyers
- Birthday announcements

These types of emails help to keep buyers engaged and connected to the brand. It is important to develop healthy relationships with buyers and not just focus on sales. B2B buyers are not likely to switch providers and change their work processes frequently.

---

[53] https://www.invespcro.com/blog/customer-acquisition-retention/

By sending these types of emails, it can help reel buyers in and get them to commit to the brand. Additionally, these emails can also be used for sales tactics such as offering a limited discount on a brand's birthday or anniversary.

Spring Clean Your Email Lists

Do you want to achieve an astounding 60% open rate[54] like Andrea Bosoni, the founder of Zero to Marketing?

Then you need to maintain and clean your email list to improve the performance of your B2B email marketing campaign. This includes removing subscribers who are no longer engaging with your emails, as this can lead to lower spam complaints, lower bounce, and unsubscribe rates, higher open and click-through rates, and improved email marketing analytics.

Signs that it may be time to remove subscribers from your list include declining open and CTR rates, increasing unsubscribe rates, high bounce rates, many spam complaints, and poor deliverability.

Take Advantage of Hot Topics

To be successful in B2B email marketing, it's important to take advantage of timely events and relevant content. (Read Part Two: Crafting Killer Content).

This can help you gain authority and credibility, catch your audience's attention, prove your brand's knowledge and understanding of the industry, and add value to your audience. To do this, it's important to stay informed about industry trends and be able to quickly act on information that affects your sector.

---

[54] https://www.indiehackers.com/product/zero-to-marketing/worked-hard-to-improve-my-email-open-rate--MA5NZTZ2wfOEPnaowql

When choosing relevant content, consider factors such as how it adds value to your audience, how it relates to your business or industry, the best way to relay the information, and any additional resources that can be included. While not every opportunity will present itself, by staying ahead of industry trends, you can capitalise on them when they do.

Don't Hesitate to Send Other People's Content

By sending your email subscribers content created by others, you show that your priority is providing them with valuable and high-quality information. It also allows you to share valuable content without having to spend time creating it yourself. Additionally, sharing content created by others can help you build relationships with other websites and brands. It goes without saying that you must be sure the content is very valuable to your target audience!

Experiment with Different "From" Address

The idea behind using different 'from' addresses in your email marketing is to build rapport with your subscribers by personalising the communication and making it feel like it's coming from a real person, rather than a generic company email.

This can be done by sending emails from multiple members of your team, rather than just one person. This approach can be effective in building trust and engagement with your subscribers, as it gives them the sense that there are real people behind the brand who care about their needs.

Additionally, it allows you to highlight different aspects of your company and the unique roles and expertise of your team members, which can add value to your subscribers.

Add P.S.

Hotmail, a company that grew rapidly in the late 1990s, used a strategy of adding P.S. I love you for helping them go from a small company to a $400 million company in just 18 months[55].

"As a way to stimulate growth, the Hotmail team added the intriguing bit of text "PS I love you" at the bottom of every email they sent, with a link back to their homepage. In less than a year, this little piece of content was responsible (in part) for their massive growth of more than 12 million email accounts"[56].
GetVero

I am not suggesting that you send I Love You to all your prospects. Instead, use P.S. to:

- Create urgency
- Provide CTR
- Share an extra thought
- Make connections
- Promote a Bonus

Automatically Send Second Email to Non-Openers with a new Subject Line

Automatically sending a second email to non-openers after 2-3 days with a different subject line can be an effective strategy to double open rates.

This approach allows you to reach out to those who may have missed or overlooked the first email and gives them another opportunity to engage with your content.

---

[55] https://www.basicthinking.com/growth-hack-hotmail/
[56] https://www.getvero.com/resources/email-marketing-hacks/

By using a different subject line, you can also pique their curiosity and encourage them to open the email. Additionally, sending a follow-up email after a few days can increase the chances of the email being seen, as it allows enough time for the recipient to clear out their inbox and for the original email to be forgotten.

This technique can also help to increase the engagement with your brand and increase conversions.

TOOLS FOR B2B EMAIL MARKETING

ActiveCampaign

ActiveCampaign is a widely popular email marketing automation tool that is not only packed with features but also affordable and easy to use. This combination of features and ease of use has made it the go-to choice for small businesses, with over 150,000 paying customers. One of the most highly-rated features of ActiveCampaign is its visual marketing automation builder, which offers 135+ triggers and actions to choose from, allowing you to easily create effective marketing sequences that combine email, SMS, push notifications, and site messages.

Additionally, ActiveCampaign offers 500+ pre-built automation recipes for those who are new to marketing automation or looking for inspiration. However, what sets ActiveCampaign apart from premium alternatives like HubSpot is its optimization features.

While all email marketing tools allow you to A/B test the basics such as email content, subject lines, and in most cases, send time, ActiveCampaign goes a step further by allowing you to split test different paths within a marketing automation sequence. This means you can test the effectiveness of different variations of emails, such as the number of emails sent or the combination of email and SMS, and then use predictive modelling to determine which variations perform best. ActiveCampaign also allows you to track goals and see the impact of different emails, marketing sequences, and split tests on conversion rate and conversion time.

MailChimp

Mailchimp is a widely popular email marketing platform that offers a range of features for businesses and individuals to create, send, and manage email marketing campaigns. It is known for its easy-to-use interface, making it a great option for beginners and small businesses. Mailchimp offers a variety of email templates, a drag-and-drop email designer, and a variety of integrations with other platforms, such as Shopify and Salesforce.

Additionally, it provides a suite of tools for targeting and segmenting audiences, analysing and optimising campaigns, and automating email sends. Mailchimp also offers a free plan that allows businesses to send up to 12,000 emails to 2,000 subscribers per month, making it a cost-effective solution for businesses with smaller lists. Overall, Mailchimp is a powerful and versatile email marketing platform that provides a wide range of features for businesses to create and manage email campaigns that increase engagement and drive revenue.

Hubspot

HubSpot offers an all-in-one platform that combines a CRM, website builder, and email marketing platform. By linking your marketing, website, and sales activity, it can identify which campaigns are driving sales. This allows you to focus on what works and reduce spending on what doesn't. The platform is well-suited for businesses that offer high-value services, as even small improvements in sales can lead to significant increases in revenue. The visual editor is user-friendly and allows you to easily create landing pages, forms, and email campaigns. The platform also offers advanced features such as personalization tokens and the ability to conditionally display content based on contact information. The automation workflow builder is easy to use and offers a wide range of actions and conditions to build sequences. However, it does not have a native A/B testing feature for running split path tests within automation sequences, but it can be added by installing an additional app.

Marketo

Marketo is a leading marketing automation software that helps businesses streamline their marketing efforts, automate tasks, and improve their ROI. It is particularly well-suited for B2B companies, as it offers a wide range of features for lead generation, lead management, and customer engagement. Marketo's platform includes tools for email marketing, lead nurturing, and lead scoring, as well as a CRM integration and a web personalization feature. The platform also includes a marketing calendar, a web analytics tool, and a landing page builder, which makes it easier to create and optimise campaigns. Additionally, Marketo offers a variety of integrations with other platforms such as Salesforce, Google Analytics, and LinkedIn, allowing businesses to easily connect their existing tools and data. Marketo's platform is known for its flexibility and scalability, making it a great choice for businesses of all sizes, from small start-ups to large enterprises. Overall, Marketo is a comprehensive marketing automation platform that offers a wide range of features to help businesses streamline their marketing efforts, automate tasks, and improve their ROI.

PART SEVEN:

EXPLORING OTHER INNOVATIVE

TACTICS

INTRODUCTION

In this part, we will look into a variety of impactful tactics. Drawing from my personal experience, these methods come in various forms and can be customised to fit the unique needs of your business.

Whether it's through physical events, website pages, or other means, this section will cover areas that were not previously discussed in the earlier chapters. So, let's dive in and explore other B2B innovative marketing tactics.

PHYSICAL EVENTS

Prospecting Days

Marketing can collaborate with sales leaders to run a full day focused on bringing new leads into the sales pipeline, or work on ageing leads with a monthly prospecting day. Not only does this boost the pipeline, but it also fosters teamwork and camaraderie among the sales and marketing teams. Marketing's job is to add a touch of gamification that can add energy and excitement to the event.

Block off a dedicated day in advance for prospecting, with no other commitments or meetings. Aim to make this event repeatable. Ideally, choose a theme to add fun and make it easier to select games or activities. Prepare a list of targeted prospects in advance, considering factors such as the industry, the product or solution focus, and whether they are cold leads, or stagnant leads, for example. Use games or activities and offer prizes to increase motivation and enjoyment.

Plan for breaks, refreshments, lunch, and possibly team drinks at the end of the day. Have a script prepared for the content of your calls and how to respond to different objections. Consider reaching out to prospects beforehand to introduce your company and product. Aim to speak with decision makers at the prospect company. Keep track of progress using post-Its, a whiteboard, or an online dashboard.

By focusing on specific themes, such as a current campaign or dormant leads, you can fine-tune your efforts and achieve better results. Here are a few additional pieces of information to inspire you.

B2B Data Providers

B2B data providers, also known as B2B contact databases, are large collections of information that businesses can access to find qualified potential customers for their sales team. You can refer to these tools when planning for your prospecting day.

These databases often contain a range of data points, including firmographic data (such as company revenue, company size, and funding amount), demographic data (such as job titles, years of experience, and location), and technographic data (such as software used by a company).

A well-designed B2B contact database allows users to search for prospects that meet specific criteria using these data points. After selecting the desired search criteria, the database will provide a list of matching prospects and often includes contact information such as email addresses and phone numbers.

Using these tools to prepare for Prospecting Days will prove to be very valuable.

Here are a few B2B Data Providers to Power Your Data Discovery and Enrichment:

1. Apollo.io or ZoomInfo

    Pricey but powerful B2B contact database and intent data provider for outreach teams. You can start with the free trial and access a limited number of contacts.

2. UpLead - B2B database with built-in email verification tools for improved contact data accuracy.

3. DemandScience Intelligence - B2B data provider combining contact details with intent data to find in-market leads.

4. Lead411 - Reliable and affordable B2B contact database for building prospect lists and staying up to date on prospect company updates.

5. BuiltWith - Find prospects based on the web technologies they use.

6. Lusha - A strong contact database and Chrome extension for prospecting across LinkedIn and company websites.

7. DiscoverOrg - B2B intelligence and contact data platform for teams running advanced outreach strategies.

8. InsideView - Powerful prospecting and data platform for teams running ABM campaigns.

9. AngelList - Directory to identify start-ups that are growing and

hiring.

10. 10.Hunter.io - Find the email address for any professional.

Capture Intent Data and Reach Out to Them

Intent data is information about a company's behaviour that indicates they are in the process of making a purchase. This can include signals such as tech changes, new job openings, new hires, funding announcements, new partnerships, product launches, awards, and expansions into new markets.

By tracking these signals, you can identify potential leads for cold outreach and tailor your messaging to their specific needs and interests.

For example, if a company is hiring in a specific department, it may be a sign that they are looking to invest more in that area of their business and could be interested in products related to that field.

Similarly, if a company is adopting new software or launching a new product, it may indicate that they are looking to grow their market share in that area and may be open to considering complementary products.

By tracking these signals and using tools like Predictleads and Bombora to gather intent data, you can identify potential leads and plan your prospecting day around your outreach that is tailored to their specific needs and interests.

Scrape Emails from Slack Groups

To gather email addresses of members from relevant Slack groups, you can use a tool like Phantombuster to scrape the groups and extract the emails of their members. Note that not all groups display the emails of their members, so this method may not work for all groups. The Phantombuster tool can automate this process and make it more efficient.

Contact Unhappy Customers of Competitors

To potentially attract new users to your product, consider reaching out to individuals who have left negative feedback about competing products on review sites like G2 or Capterra. These users may be open to hearing about an alternative solution to their problem that was not adequately addressed by the competing product.

To help identify unhappy users of competitor products, you can use tools like Visualping.io to monitor review sites for new negative reviews. By contacting these users and offering them a better solution to their needs, you may be able to attract new customers to your product.

Host an Ask me Anything (AMA) with your Senior Executive/ Visiting Senior Leadership

"Ask Me Anything" (AMA) sessions and panel discussions are excellent ways to build relationships with your audience and customers. These conversational formats allow you to engage with your audience in a more informal setting, providing valuable insights and information about your product, business, and journey.

AMA sessions can be conducted in person over cocktails, lunch, or other social events, or they can be held online. Either way, these sessions offer a truly audience-driven experience, allowing participants to ask questions and discuss hot topics within your industry.

Executive Roundtables

Executive roundtables are important for B2B marketing because they provide a forum for top executives from different companies to come together and discuss key issues and challenges facing their industries.

These roundtables can be an effective way for businesses to build relationships with key decision-makers, learn about the latest trends and developments in their industry, and identify new opportunities for growth and collaboration.

For B2B marketers, participating in CXO roundtables can be a valuable way to showcase their expertise, build credibility, and establish themselves as thought leaders in their field.

By engaging with other executives and sharing insights and best practices, B2B marketers can position their company as a valuable resource for their target audience and build trust with potential customers.

Executive roundtables can be challenging to organise, but with careful planning and execution, they can be highly successful. Here are four ideas for ensuring that your executive roundtable is a success:

1) Recruit anchor attendees who are executives that you already have a strong relationship with. This will help ensure that you have a solid foundation of high-level participants.

2) Work with a media group, such as media publications, to promote the event and attract a broader audience.

3) Partner with analysts to provide recent research reports that can inform discussions and provide valuable insights.

4) Consider working with a consulting partner and committing to each bringing five anchor executive attendees.

5) Finally, you can hire an agency who specialises in drawing executive attendees. By partnering with a specialised agency, you can ensure that your event appeals to this targeted audience. These agencies have the expertise to guide you in developing an effective format and relevant content that will resonate with senior executives, helping to increase attendance and engagement at your event.

By following these strategies, you can create a strong foundation for a successful and impactful executive roundtable.

KEEP THIS IN MIND

The Gold is in the Follow Up

Remember that securing the attendance of high-level executives to your events is only the first step.

To ensure conversion, it's crucial to have a strong follow-up structure in place. Work with your sales team, agree on assigning each executive attendee to a dedicated sales representative or senior executive for personalised follow-up.

Provide attendees (and no-shows) with a summary of the event and any relevant materials, and schedule additional touchpoints, such as follow-up events, to continue building relationships and driving conversions.

A Partner Summit

Hosting an annual partner summit can be a powerful way for B2B marketers looking to strengthen relationships with their partners and drive business growth. An annual partner summit is a gathering of your company's strategic partners, typically held once a year, to discuss business goals, share best practices, and explore new opportunities for collaboration.

These events can be an effective way to showcase your company's products and services, build trust and credibility with partners, and stay up to date on industry trends and developments. In addition to providing valuable content and networking opportunities for attendees, an annual partner summit can also be a great way to demonstrate your commitment to your partnerships and drive long-term growth for your business.

As a bonus, top partners can be recognized and celebrated at the summit, further strengthening the relationship, and fostering loyalty.

TIP: Get Top Target Customers to Be a Guest Speaker at Your Events

While it is common practice to invite existing customers to speak at company-led events, to establish valuable connections, consider extending the invitation to top target customers as well. Not only will this demonstrate your interest in positioning them as thought leaders in their industry, but it also presents a unique opportunity to build relationships and open the door to potential collaborations or sales opportunities. You might be surprised at how many of these top prospects will agree to speak, especially when you approach them with a personalised and meaningful opportunity.

WEBSITE

Prominently Display Customer Reviews

Having customer reviews prominently displayed on your website or landing page is crucial for attracting buyers and can play a major role in your B2B marketing strategy.

According to a TrustRadius report, a significant percentage of younger generations rely on review sites as the first step in their buying journey. Without reviews, potential customers may have a hard time making informed decisions about purchasing your product for their business. Furthermore, software products with 10 or more reviews tend to see a significant increase in website traffic and higher click-through rates for PPC campaigns. Continuously adding reviews to your product profile can lead to positive results for your business.

Offer an ROI Calculator

Adding an ROI (return on investment) calculator to your B2B website can be a good idea for several reasons:

1. It helps to demonstrate the value of your products or services: By showing potential customers how much they can expect to gain from using your products or services, you can help to justify the cost and persuade them to make a purchase.

2. It can improve the user experience: An ROI calculator can provide valuable information to visitors, which can help them to make more informed decisions about whether to invest in your products or services.

3. It can provide useful data: An ROI calculator can also provide valuable data about what your customers are looking for and how much they are willing to invest. This can help you to tailor your marketing efforts more effectively and optimise your sales strategy.

4. It can increase conversions: By providing a clear and concise way

to calculate the potential return on investment, you can increase the chances that visitors will take the desired action, such as filling out a form or making a purchase.

Adding an ROI calculator to your B2B website can be a valuable marketing tool that helps to demonstrate the value of your products or services, improve the user experience, provide useful data, and increase conversions.

An online calculator can serve as a useful tool for generating leads and providing valuable information to both your sales team and your customers. When visitors input their information into a calculator, they become identified as potential prospects who are interested in exploring whether your product or service meets their needs.

This information can help your sales team have more productive initial conversations with these prospects. At the same time, customers can gain a better understanding of your offerings and the potential benefits of working with your team. Many calculators are designed to illustrate cost savings for prospective clients, demonstrating the annualised return on investment that they can expect from working with your team. By establishing this baseline early on, subsequent sales conversations can be more targeted and productive.

Pricing Page

It is possible that adding a pricing page to a website without disclosing the actual price may increase the number of inbounds for a B2B company because it allows potential customers to express interest in the company's products or services without committing to a purchase.

This approach may be particularly effective for B2B companies that offer customised or complex products or services, as it allows them to gather more information about the potential customer's needs before providing a quote.

By requiring interested parties to request a meeting or consultation, the company can have a more targeted and personalised conversation with the potential customer, which may be more effective in converting leads into sales. Additionally, this approach may also help to filter out less qualified leads, as it requires potential customers to take an active step in expressing their interest.

Offer a Free Tool

Offering a free tool as a B2B marketing tactic can be an effective way to attract and engage potential customers. By providing a valuable resource that meets the needs of your target audience, you can establish your brand as an authority in your industry and generate interest in your products or services.

There are a few different ways you can use a free tool to drive traffic and generate leads for your business. One approach is to create a standalone tool that addresses a specific problem or need for your audience. For example, you could create a tool that helps businesses calculate their return on investment for a particular marketing campaign, or that helps them generate ideas for blog post titles. By promoting the tool through your website, social media channels, and other marketing channels, you can attract many visitors and drive traffic to your site.

Another option is to buy a code for a pre-existing tool and white label it as your own. This can be a cost-effective way to offer a valuable resource to your audience without having to invest a lot of time and resources into developing the tool from scratch. There are several websites, such as Codecanyon, where you can purchase code for a variety of different tools at a relatively low cost. By white labelling the tool and promoting it as your own, you can still generate value for your business while saving time and resources.

Regardless of which approach you take, it's important to ensure that your free tool is high-quality and useful to your audience. This will help you establish your brand as a trusted source of information and may lead to increased engagement and conversions for your business.

OTHERS:

A Referral Program

Nothing quite matches the value of a direct referral! Let's explore some compelling statistics related to Referrals in B2B published in a 2023 report by ThinkImpact[57] :

- 83% of customers are open to referring a business after conducting a successful purchase.
- 78% of the B2B referrals create viable customer leads for the business.
- Just 3 in very 10 B2B businesses have a formalised referral business.
- Referrals end up creating 65% of new business opportunities.
- Referred B2B customers have a 37% higher retention rate than acquired clients.

When decision-makers in B2B companies receive recommendations from people they trust, they are more likely to listen and consider making a purchase.

Referral marketing is an effective tactic for B2B businesses to attract new customers and grow their customer base.

If your business only informally emails or calls customers to ask them to refer to your brand, that doesn't count as a referral program.

Instead, B2B referral programs involve a streamlined referral page where clients enter their peer's information and easily refer them to your business.

It involves a formalised process where satisfied customers, (but also employees, prospects, or partners) recommend your brand to decision-makers at other businesses. Customers can be incentivized for every opportunity that is confirmed by Sales or when a deal is closed.

---

[57] https://www.thinkimpact.com/b2b-referral-statistics/

> **TIP:** Ensure all customer facing teams, including your sales and customer success teams support the initiative. Include the referral page link or QR Code on their slides.
>
> Keep the program open not just for existing customers, but also prospects, partners, and potential partners.

To create a successful B2B referral program, it's important to make it easy for clients to share your brand, design a simple lead form and include a clear call to action, use a referral code or link, personalise the referral's experience, craft a compelling referral message, choose an incentive that motivates your customers, and promote your program.

Automating your referral program with B2B referral software such as Growsurf or CustomerGauge and tracking your referral marketing goals can also help ensure its success.

Run a Campaign to Collect Reviews

Online reviews and referrals have become increasingly crucial for businesses as buyers now tend to research products and services online before making a purchase.

Not only do they help to build trust and loyalty between a business and its customers, but they also hold added weight in the B2B context where the decision-makers are trying to spend someone else's money.

A study conducted by G2 Crowd and Heinz Marketing found that 92% of B2B buyers are more likely to make a purchase after reading a trusted review[58].

Collecting B2B software reviews can be a challenge. Here are several smart and easy ways to do it.

1. One way is to send an email blast to your customers, asking for a review and including a direct link to your reviews form. You can send the email to all of your customers or a specific segment or subset of them.

---

[58] https://learn.g2.com/consumer-reviews

2. Another way is to add a review call-to-action in your regular customer newsletter, which reminds your customers that you appreciate their feedback.
3. Use marketing automation software to create an email nurture program for new customers and ask them to leave a review after a specific amount of time has passed.
4. If you are a software company, leveraging your software system is also a good idea, by including a call-to-action on the login page or main dashboard.
5. Social media is another great way to reach your customers and promote current reviews and direct links to pages where customers can write a new review.
6. User events and conferences can be a great opportunity to collect many reviews in a short amount of time.
7. Use a third-party review service that can make it easy for your customers to leave reviews.
8. Offer incentives such as discounts or rewards for customers who leave reviews.
9. Leverage your customer support team to ask for reviews after resolving an issue.
10. Send a follow-up email to customers who have recently purchased your product, asking for a review.
11. Offer a survey or feedback form for customers to fill out and use the responses to improve your product and then ask for a review.
12. Leverage your sales team to ask for reviews from happy customers during the sales process.

By using a combination of these tactics, you can increase the chances of getting more reviews from your customers and ultimately improve your sales and marketing efforts.

Create a Course

Consider creating a course by organising and presenting your B2B seminars in a structured format. By doing so, you can establish yourself as a subject matter expert in a particular topic and provide a valuable resource for those interested in learning about it.

Additionally, offering a certificate of completion can serve as a validation of the knowledge and skills gained by those who complete the course. This can also lead to increased visibility and credibility, as those who receive the certificate may be proud to share it on social media and potentially attract new participants to the course.

Offer a Full-Service Migration

To attract new users and make it easier for them to switch to your product from a competitor's, offer a full-service migration process.

This will help users quickly onboard your product and start using it right away.

This will help users reach the activation point sooner and encourage them to continue using your product. By providing a seamless migration process, you can make it easier for users to switch to your product and ensure that they have a positive experience from the start.

Deliver Unforgettable Webinars by Emulating TV Shows

Emulating TV shows when running webinars for B2B can be a great way to engage and entertain your audience while also delivering valuable information and promoting your products or services. There are a few key strategies you can use to emulate TV shows when running webinars:

1. Use visually appealing graphics and slides: Just like TV shows use graphics and on-screen text to convey information and keep viewers engaged, you can use visually appealing graphics and slides in your webinar to convey important points and keep your audience interested.

2. Use video segments: TV shows often use video segments to break up the action and keep viewers engaged. You can do the same by incorporating video segments into your webinar, whether it's a recorded demo of your product, an interview with an industry expert, or a case study from a satisfied customer.

3. Use interactive elements: TV shows often use interactive elements,

such as polls and quizzes, to keep viewers engaged and involved. You can use these same techniques in your webinar by incorporating polls, quizzes, and other interactive elements to encourage audience participation and keep them engaged.

4. Use a consistent format: TV shows often have a consistent format that viewers can rely on, and you can do the same by establishing a consistent format for your webinars. This might include a set agenda, a consistent length, and a regular schedule.

By using these strategies, you can effectively emulate TV shows when running webinars for B2B, engaging, and entertaining your audience while also delivering valuable information and promoting your products or services.

Cross Promotion

Cross promotion is a marketing strategy where two businesses with complementary products or services agree to promote each other's products to their respective audiences. In B2B marketing, cross promotion can be an effective way to reach new customers and expand your reach, especially if you partner with a non-competing company that has the same target audience as your business.

There are several ways that B2B businesses can use cross promotion to their advantage:

1. Joint webinars or events: Host a joint webinar or event with your partner company, where you can both promote your products or services to a shared audience.

2. Social media promotion: Share each other's content on social media platforms and encourage your followers to follow your partner company.

3. Email marketing campaigns: Include information about your partner company's products or services in your email marketing campaigns and encourage your subscribers to check them out.

4. Affiliate marketing programs: Set up an affiliate marketing program with your partner company, where you can earn commissions by promoting their products to your audience.

Cross promotion can be a valuable marketing strategy for B2B businesses looking to reach new customers and expand their reach. By partnering with a non-competing company that has the same target audience, you can effectively promote your products or services to a wider audience and achieve your business goals.

PART EIGHT:

MASTERING CONVERSION OPTIMISATION

INTRODUCTION

"Conversion rate optimization results in highly-qualified leads, increased revenue, and lower acquisition costs."[59]

HubSpot

Measuring the marketing conversion rate is an essential KPI for B2B marketers as it indicates how well your marketing efforts and product are resonating with the audience, and how effectively they are driving the desired action. It's also important to track the sales conversion rate, as it ultimately reflects the success of all the marketing efforts in terms of actual sales made.

Some people may see the conversion rate as something that simply happens, but it's important to set specific, informed goals for it and understand what a "good" conversion rate looks like.

What is conversion rate optimization and why is it important?

Conversion optimization in B2B marketing is the process of increasing the number of website visitors who take a desired action, such as filling out a form, signing up for a newsletter, or making a purchase. This is important because it helps businesses convert more leads into paying customers, which ultimately leads to increased revenue and growth.

In B2B marketing, the process of conversion optimization can be especially crucial because the sales cycles are often longer, and the decision-making process is more complex than in B2C marketing.

By understanding and optimising the customer journey, B2B marketers can increase the chances of turning website visitors into qualified leads and ultimately closing deals. Additionally, tracking and analysing conversion rates can provide valuable insights into how well marketing strategies are performing and where improvements can be made

---

[59] https://blog.hubspot.com/marketing/conversion-rate-optimization-guide

TIP: When it comes to conversion rates, it's essential to keep in mind that industry benchmarks can vary significantly. Factors such as the products and services offered, and the marketing channels used can greatly impact this number. To effectively optimise your B2B conversion rate, it's crucial to compare your rate to that of other companies in your industry and determine if you are meeting industry standards. Additionally, it's important to consider regional variations when analysing conversion rates. By keeping these factors in mind, you can gain a better understanding of your company's performance and identify areas for improvement.

TACTICS TO IMPROVE CONVERSION RATES ACROSS THE FUNNEL

Conversion Optimisation on Search or Ads

Add Star Ratings in Google Search and Ad Description

Adding Star Ratings in Search Engine Results Page (SERP) and Google Ads improves CTRs (Click Through Ratios) from Google search results and ads by implementing star ratings. Reviews = credibility.

There are several reasons why B2B marketers should consider adding star ratings in their ad descriptions:

1. Star ratings can help increase the credibility and trustworthiness of an ad. Consumers are more likely to trust a product or service with high ratings, and this can translate to increased conversions for B2B marketers.

2. Star ratings can help differentiate your product or service from competitors. If your product has high ratings compared to similar products, this can make it stand out to potential customers.

3. Star ratings can help improve the visibility of an ad. Some search engines and platforms use ratings as a factor in their ranking algorithms, so including ratings in your ad can improve its visibility and reach.

4. Star ratings can help increase the engagement with an ad. Customers are more likely to click on and interact with an ad that includes ratings, which can lead to increased engagement and conversions.

Adding star ratings in your ad description can help improve the credibility, differentiation, visibility, and engagement of your ad, leading to increased success for your B2B marketing efforts

Here is a video on how to add Review Stars to your Search Engine Result page (SERP) Listings. (https://www.smamarketing.net/blog/how-to-add-review-stars-to-your-serp-listings)

Optimise Your Meta Descriptions

Did you know that according to <u>Ahrefs' research</u>, only 74.98% of top-ranking pages have meta descriptions[60]? This is a very big, missed opportunity for 25.02% to rank higher in search results!

Meta descriptions, also called search descriptions, are a short summary of up to 155 characters that appears in the HTML code of a webpage and describes the content of the page. Search engines display the meta description underneath the page title in search results when the searched phrase appears in the description. They are like a pitch that convinces the user that the page is exactly what they're looking for.

Even if using a keyword in the meta description doesn't improve search rankings, it may help grab a searcher's attention.

To make the most of meta descriptions, use them to introduce your brand and clearly communicate the value or information that users will find on your page.

By including your brand name and a compelling description of what users can expect to find on your page, you can appeal to a larger audience and encourage more people to follow the link to your website.

> **TIP:** Make sure the meta description includes the targeted keywords, clearly and effectively describes your page's content (show what's in it for them and includes a call to action. Extra points if you can make it unique!

Here is a great example from www.monsterinsights.com

> *Monsterinsights - The Best Google Analytics Plugin for Wordpress*
>
> *Monsterinsights is the best Google Analytics plugin for Wordpress, Set up Google Analytics for WordPress with just a few clicks. Over 100 million downloads.*

---

[60] https://aioseo.com/how-to-write-meta-descriptions-for-seo/

Boost Your Click-Through-Ratio (CTR) by Using Google Ad's Geo Ad Customizers

Google Ads offers two features called Geo Ad Customizers that allow you to personalise your ad copy based on the location of each search, without having to create separate campaigns for each city or state. This can be especially useful for businesses that provide localised services. Geo Ad Customizers allow you to dynamically change your ad copy based on the searcher's location, which can improve click-through rate (CTR) and engagement with your ads.

To set up Geo Ad Customizers, you'll need to decide on the ad copy you want to use for each location you are targeting. For example, you might offer a face-to-face demo in certain locations or provide a service in specific cities. Once you have decided on your ad copy, you can follow the instructions provided by Google Ads to set up your customizers.

Conversion Optimisation on Website or Landing Pages

A Double CTA

Having a double call to action (CTA) can be a powerful marketing strategy that can help businesses achieve their goals. Here are some benefits of using a double CTA:

1. Increased conversions: A double CTA gives your audience two opportunities to act, which can increase the chances of them converting.

2. Greater flexibility: A double CTA allows you to present two different options to your audience, giving them the choice to select the one that best fits their needs or interests. A client may not be ready to speak to your salesperson but would be more inclined to watch a customer testimonial. Or ask questions before a free trial.

3. Better targeting: By offering two different CTAs, you can tailor your message to different segments of your audience and increase the likelihood that they will act.

4. Greater engagement: A double CTA can help keep your audience engaged and encourage them to continue exploring your website or product.

5. Improved customer experience: A double CTA can help improve the overall customer experience by providing them with more options and allowing them to choose the path that best fits their needs.

Balance Calls-to-Action with Calls-to-Value

Common Call to Action (CTA) buttons are "learn more," "download now," and "get started," which rely on header copy to provide essential context. A call-to-value (CTV), on the other hand, is a type of call-to-action that includes a value proposition and helps to reinforce the benefits of an offer.

CTVs can be effective in convincing leads to make a purchase, especially when used in conjunction with body copy that explains the value of the product or service. In contrast, a call-to-action (CTA) is typically used for individuals who have already decided to buy a product or service and just need to know what to do next.

CTA buttons should be straightforward and clear, as they are meant to facilitate the final step in the purchasing process. It can be beneficial to use a mixture of CTVs and CTAs in marketing materials to effectively engage and convert leads.

- Access our Members Only Library & Start Learning
- Yes, send me more Useful Tips
- See our work
- Explore our portfolio

Negative Opt-Outs

Using negative opt-outs in pop-ups can be effective in increasing the number of users who choose a positive option, but it should be approached with caution. These opt-outs are options that present a negative scenario, such as "no, I already have a lot of money" or "no, my website already gets a ton of traffic."

When users see these options, they may not want to be associated with the negative scenario and will be more likely to choose the positive option. However, it's important to be careful with this tactic as overusing it can make users feel bad about themselves.

Put Difficult Signup Steps to the End

To increase sign-up completion rates, prioritise easy-to-fill form fields at the beginning of the process and save the riskier or more time-consuming steps for later. This takes advantage of the cognitive bias called completion bias, where people feel a strong desire to finish a task once they have started it. Our brains are wired to seek the pleasure of completing a task. By moving the more difficult steps to the end, you can capitalise on this natural inclination and improve your sign-up rates.

Use Autofill for Form Fields

To make it easier for users to complete forms on your website, you can use a tool like Clearbit Forms to automatically fill in form fields based on enriched data. This can save users time and effort, as they won't have to type out all the information themselves.

However, it's important to still provide an option for users to edit the form input if they want to, as this allows them to make any necessary corrections or updates.

By providing an autofill feature and still allowing users to edit the form input, you can help increase the number of users who complete the form and provide the information you are seeking.

Self-Qualification

Self-qualification is a marketing strategy where visitors to a website or business are asked to answer a series of questions in order to determine if they are a good fit for a particular product or service. This is often done in the form of a quiz.

The goal of self-qualification is to establish trust with potential customers by only offering products or services that meet their specific needs, rather than trying to sell them anything at all costs. By doing this, businesses can create a more personalised and targeted marketing approach and build a stronger relationship with their customers.

In-Line Validation Technique

In-line validation is a technique for providing feedback to users as they fill out a form. Instead of waiting until the user clicks the submit button to display any errors, in-line validation delivers messages to the user in real-time based on whether the information they have entered is correct or incorrect. This helps to improve the user experience by allowing users to fix errors as they go, rather than having to go back and fix them all at once after submitting the form. However, it's important to be careful when using in-line validation, as displaying error messages before the user has finished typing can be confusing and annoying.

Add a Priming Step

To make the signup process more effective, you can consider adding a priming step at the beginning. This step involves explaining to users why they need to fill out the form and what they will receive in return.

This additional step can make the process feel less cumbersome to users, as it reassures them and helps them feel more comfortable proceeding with the rest of the process. By adding this step, you can help increase the chances of successful signups.

Don't Make Forms Look Like Forms

To make forms more appealing to users, try to make them look less like forms. One way to do this is to use large, clickable images and toggle sliders, which can make filling out the form feel more interactive and enjoyable.

By making forms more visually appealing and interactive, you can increase the chances that users will complete them and provide the information you are seeking. It's important to remember that people generally don't like filling out forms, so anything you can do to make the process more enjoyable will likely be appreciated by users.

Upfront Progress

One way to encourage users to complete a task is to show them the progress they have already made. This can help motivate them to finish the task because they feel a higher need to complete it as it gets closer to completion. On the Internet, you can show progress in several ways, such as by displaying a crossed-out item on an onboarding checklist, or by showing a 50% complete bar on a popup after a user has only clicked it once.

The key is to make sure that users feel the progress as soon as possible, so they are motivated to continue. This technique can be particularly effective for tasks that may seem daunting or time-consuming, as it helps to break the task down into smaller, more manageable steps.

Social Proof Next to Friction Points

Placing social proof elements next to points of friction on your website can help to decrease the psychological resistance that visitors experience when trying to complete an action, such as filling out a form or clicking a call-to-action button. Social proof refers to the influence that the actions and opinions of others have on our own behaviour. By showing visitors that others have successfully completed the same action, you can help to reduce their resistance and increase the chances that they will take the desired action.

Examples of social proof elements that you might include on your website include customer logos, the number of users you have, testimonials, awards or certifications, press mentions, and ratings from app stores or user review sites like Capterra. By incorporating these types of elements into your website design, you can help to build trust and credibility with visitors and encourage them to take the desired action.

Pricing Page GIFs

One way to increase signups on your pricing page is to add GIFs to the tooltips for your pricing plans. This can help users better understand your product's features without having to leave the page. An example of this tactic in action can be seen at https://blackmagic.so/membership/.

Quiz in Exit Pop Up

To increase engagement with your exit-intent pop-up, consider including a quiz that asks a few relevant questions and then requests an email to send the result.

The most effective quiz pop-ups are typically related to the content of the page on which they appear. For example, a blog post about analytics could include a quiz testing visitors' knowledge of Google Analytics, while a post about conversion rate optimization (CRO) could include a CRO knowledge quiz.

This approach can help capture email addresses and increase engagement with your website.

Don't Hide Short Forms Behind Buttons

Instead of hiding short forms behind buttons, place them directly on your pages. This allows visitors to see how easy the forms are to fill out and may encourage them to complete the form.

Hiding the forms can make it more difficult for visitors to see the value in filling them out and may discourage them from completing the form. By placing the forms directly on your pages, you can make it easier for visitors to access and complete them.

Match Call to Action Copy to Blog Posts

To increase the number of signups from your blog, consider using specific, contextual call-to-action (CTA) copy that aligns with the content of each blog post.

Instead of using generic CTAs across your entire blog, try to tailor your CTAs to the specific topic or challenge addressed in each post. This can help make readers more confident that your product is the right solution for their needs and increase the likelihood that they will convert. By matching the CTA copy to the content of each blog post, you can create a more targeted and effective call to action that resonates with your readers and encourages them to take the next step.

Match Search Intent with Content Upgrades

To improve the effectiveness of your content upgrades and increase the conversion rate of your forms, consider aligning the search intent of your users with the content you offer. One way to do this is by using Google

Search Console to identify the specific phrases that users searched for to find your page. By understanding the specific information that users are seeking, you can offer content upgrades, such as PDF downloads, that are closely related to their needs.

This targeted approach is more likely to be successful than a generic call-to-action or newsletter subscription form, as it addresses the specific needs and interests of your users.

By aligning your content upgrades with the search intent of your users, you can improve the conversion rate of your forms and effectively capture the contact information of your target audience.

Add Interactive Quizzes in Blogs

One way to generate more leads from your blog posts is to embed interactive quizzes that engage users and collect relevant information. For example, Paddle, a software company, used interactive quizzes in their blog post about churn reduction to test visitors on their churn prevention efforts.

https://paddle.com/blog/reduce-churn

The quiz asked users about the measures they take to reduce churn at their companies and collected business metrics such as MMR, growth, and churn rate.

It also collected users' email addresses and provided a score based on their inputs, along with a call-to-action (CTA) to check out Paddle's churn reduction features. By using this interactive quiz, Paddle was able to collect valuable data from users and qualify leads to move them down the funnel. Interactive quizzes can be a fun and effective way to engage users and collect relevant information for lead generation.

Breadcrumb Technique

The breadcrumb technique is a way to get visitors to take small steps or micro-conversions before asking for personal information or contact details. This can be helpful because asking for personal information can be intimidating and may cause visitors to hesitate or abandon the process.

The goal of the breadcrumb technique is to build trust and familiarity by asking easy questions that allow visitors to remain anonymous. For example, a growth agency might ask prospects about the funnel step that is most important to them now, while a software development company might ask about the scope of a project (mobile, web, or both).

This technique works best for big asks, such as requesting quotes, and can be more effective if you use dropdown or radio buttons to make it easy for visitors to answer the questions. By using the breadcrumb technique, you can gradually build trust and engagement with visitors, making it more likely that they will complete the conversion process.

Multi Step Forms

To make it feel less intimidating for users to complete long forms, consider splitting them into multiple steps.

This technique, known as using multi-step forms, can be particularly effective on mobile devices, where long forms can be more difficult to navigate.

By breaking the form into smaller, more manageable steps, you can make it easier for users to complete the form and increase the likelihood that they will finish it.

You can also use this technique to guide users through the form by providing clear instructions and displaying progress indicators, which can help improve the overall user experience. In summary, using multi-step forms can be an effective way to make long forms more manageable and increase the chances that users will complete them.

Prequalify Leads Before Sign-Up

If your product or service is not suitable for customers with low budgets or low traffic, it may be beneficial to add additional questions to your sign-up form that can help pre-qualify leads.

For example, you could include a field asking about website traffic, and set a minimum threshold that you believe potential customers must meet to have a chance of becoming actual customers. By increasing the friction at sign-up and filtering out unqualified leads, you can reduce the workload for your sales team and improve the efficiency of your sales process.

Sticky CTA Button on Mobile

To make it easier for mobile users to take the desired action on your website, consider fixing a call-to-action (CTA) button to the bottom of the screen. This will allow users to access the CTA at all times without having to scroll back to the top or bottom of the page.

By making the CTA visible and easily accessible, you can increase the chances of users clicking it and proceeding through the next steps in your sales or conversion funnel.

Upsell on Thank you Page

This is a prime opportunity to capitalise on users' engagement and inclination to take further action, as they have already demonstrated their interest and trust by completing an initial conversion. It's also advantageous as you already have their contact information, eliminating the need for them to re-enter it. This approach utilises a psychological principle known as the "foot-in-the-door" technique, which suggests that once a person has agreed to a small request, they are more likely to comply with a larger one. It is important to note that this should not be executed immediately after users sign up for your app, as the priority at that point should be to demonstrate the value of your product to them without any distractions.

Use Trust Seals

Trust seals, such as badges from reputable organisations, can provide reassurance to customers and make them feel more secure about sharing their sensitive information with you. This can lead to an increase in conversions. The effectiveness of trust seals may be greater for less well-known brands. It is recommended to choose badges that are recognizable to your target audience for the best results. Examples include badges for being PayPal Verified, McAfee Secure and so on.

Personalise your Landing Page Dynamically Based on Location

Similarly, you can boost landing page conversions by personalising its content to users' location, thereby making the content more relevant to them. This can include personalised images and copy that specifically mentions the user's location. Here is your step by step tutorial (https://www.youtube.com/watch?v=1KiGKd2XXL4&themeRefresh=1)

Landing page: Dynamic Keyword Insertion in Landing pages

This tactic involves using dynamic keyword insertion on landing pages to improve conversion rates. This technique allows you to insert the keyword that triggered an ad into the copy on the landing page, making the offer more relevant to visitors. This can be done using tools like Google Optimise or Unbounce's built-in feature.

It's important to ensure that the landing page copy matches the ad copy, as this helps to build trust with users by meeting the expectations set by the ad message. If the offer on the landing page is different from that in the ad, it may lead to a loss of trust and result in a lower conversion rate. Dynamic keyword insertion can help to ensure that the landing page offer is aligned with the ad message, helping to increase conversions.

Supercharge Your Retargeting Campaigns

To improve the performance of your retargeting campaigns, try adjusting the frequency of your ads based on the amount of time that has passed since a user visited your site. It's generally less effective to show retargeting ads to users the longer it has been since their visit, so you can optimise your campaign by dividing it into several ad groups and adjusting the frequency of each group accordingly.

For example, you might show ads with high frequency (2-3 times per day) to users who visited your site within the past week, then lower the frequency to once per day for users who visited 1-2 weeks ago, and only occasionally show ads (once every 2-3 weeks) to users who visited more than 2 weeks ago. Be sure to consider your average time to close a deal when setting the retargeting frequency to ensure that you are striking the right balance between staying top-of-mind and avoiding oversaturation.

Additionally, you should retarget Landing Pages with different messaging.

If users are visiting your custom landing page but not converting, it may be because your messaging is not resonating with them. In this case, it is unlikely that retargeting them back to the same page will be effective.

Instead, consider using a landing page with a different value proposition or a new way of explaining your product to see if it performs better. This will allow you to test different approaches and find out which messaging is most effective in convincing users to take the next step.

By experimenting with different free messaging on your landing pages, you can identify the messages that are most likely to resonate with your target audience and increase your conversion rate.

Conversions for Webinars: Try Automatic Just In-Time Webinars

To increase the percentage of signups who attend your webinar, consider offering an automatic just-in-time webinar that users can watch almost immediately. With this approach, you can pre-record the webinar and make it available on request.

Users can then select a time that is convenient for them, and the webinar will start in just a few minutes.

This approach allows users to watch the webinar at their own pace and schedule, which can help increase attendance. Additionally, you can use this approach as a lead generation tactic by offering the webinar through an exit-intent popup.

A tool like Livestorm can help you set up and manage this type of webinar. By offering an automatic just-in-time webinar, you can make it easier for users to attend and increase the chances that they will participate in the event.

Conversion Optimisation for Social Media

Pin a DM CTA Tweet

Adding a call to action (CTA) can increase your conversion rate and boost the users' engagement with your Twitter brand. Though the platform doesn't give much choice to customise a tweet, this simple hack can increase the range of tools in your belt to market your brand.

To encourage Twitter users to message you directly, pin a tweet to the top of your profile that includes a call to action (CTA) to send you a direct message (DM). To do this, you will need to make sure that you have the option to "Accept DMs from anyone" turned on. Then, follow these steps:

1. Find your numeric Twitter account ID by using TweeterID
2. Add a link to the end of your tweet that includes your Twitter ID and the desired CTA copy. The link should look something like this: https://twitter.com/messages/compose
3. Pin this tweet to the top of your profile so that it is easy for users to find and message you.

Activate LinkedIn Lead Gen Forms

Lead Generation Forms enable you to gather valuable contact information from individuals who view your LinkedIn or Showcase Page. These forms can be easily filled out and submitted by visitors with their details already pre-populated.

Conversion Optimisation after Lead Generation

Lead Nurturing

It is a well-known fact that 80% of new leads[61] do not turn into sales. Studies show that companies that effectively nurture their leads are able to generate 50% more sales-ready leads at a lower cost[62].

B2B marketers must implement lead nurturing strategies.

One of the first steps in lead nurturing is scoring the leads. This process involves assigning a score to each lead based on their level of engagement and interest in your product or service. This allows you to prioritise the leads that are most likely to convert and focus your efforts on them.

Once you have scored the leads, it's important to segment them based on their score and other characteristics such as their industry or job title. This allows you to tailor your messaging and approach to each group,

---

[61] https://www.invespcro.com/blog/lead-nurturing/
[62] https://www.invespcro.com/blog/lead-nurturing/

ensuring that you are speaking to their specific needs and pain points.

Email automation is a powerful tool for lead nurturing. By setting up automated emails that are triggered by specific actions or behaviours, you can ensure that your leads are receiving relevant and timely information. This can include welcome emails, follow-up emails after a form submission, and personalised content recommendations.

Finally, it's important to continue to encourage continuous engagement with your valuable content. This can be achieved by providing valuable resources such as whitepapers, e-books, and webinars, as well as through social media and other channels. By continuing to provide valuable content, you can keep your leads engaged and interested in your company, increasing the likelihood that they will convert into paying customers.

> **TIP:** Inbound Leads should be Followed Up Within a 24-Hour Window
>
> It is crucial for whoever handles lead processing, whether it be in marketing, sales, or SDR, to follow up on B2B leads within 24 hours.
>
> Prompt follow-up can play a vital role in turning leads into customers. According to a recent study by B2B Decision Labs , if we respond to inbound leads within 24 hours, win rates increase by 50% and about 28% of deals were over the average deal size—a 21 % increase compared to when we wait more than a day[63].

Publish a Weekly Lead Scorecard

Publishing a weekly lead scorecard can be important for B2B marketing because it allows the marketing team to track the effectiveness of their lead generation efforts and identify areas for improvement. The lead scorecard should include metrics such as the number of leads generated, the percentage of leads that are qualified, and the conversion rate of leads to customers. By regularly reviewing these metrics, the marketing team can assess the performance of their campaigns and determine whether

---

[63] https://b2bdecisionlabs.com/

they are effectively targeting the right audience and generating high-quality leads. Additionally, the lead scorecard can serve as a useful tool for improving communication and collaboration between the marketing and sales teams, as it provides both teams with a clear understanding of the status of the lead pipeline.

Similarly, Publish the Lead Aging Report

Generating a lead ageing report is equally important for a few reasons.

First, it allows you to track the progress of your lead generation efforts over time. By analysing the data in your lead ageing report, you can see how quickly you are converting leads into customers and identify any bottlenecks or challenges in the process. This can help you optimise your lead generation efforts and improve your conversion rate.

Second, a lead ageing report can help you prioritise your lead follow-up efforts. By understanding how long a lead has been in your pipeline, you can prioritise your efforts and focus on the leads that are most likely to convert. For example, you may want to prioritise leads that are newer and more engaged, as they may be more likely to convert than older, less engaged leads.

Third, a lead ageing report can help you identify trends and patterns in your lead generation efforts. By analysing the data over time, you can see which lead generation tactics are most effective, and which ones may be less effective. This can help you adjust your strategy and allocate your resources more effectively.

In summary, generating a lead ageing report is an important way to track and optimise your lead generation efforts, and helps you prioritise and identify trends and patterns.

Assign an Opportunity Sponsor for Large Opportunities

It is extremely valuable to appoint an opportunity sponsor for large deals in a B2B sales process because the opportunity sponsor serves as the primary point of contact and advocate for the deal within the organisation.

The opportunity sponsor is responsible for driving the sales process forward, coordinating efforts across departments, and ensuring that all necessary resources are brought to bear on the deal. Having a designated opportunity sponsor helps to ensure that the deal receives the necessary attention and support within the organisation and can help to avoid delays or miscommunications that could jeopardise the success of the deal. Additionally, the opportunity sponsor can serve as a trusted advisor and point of contact for the customer, helping to build strong relationships and increase the likelihood of closing the deal.

An opportunity sponsor should be appointed as soon as an active pipeline is established or the probability of a B2B sales opportunity reaches 10% or more. To begin the relationship on a positive note, the executive sponsor can send an email introducing themselves to the opportunity top champion or senior executive and offer assistance if needed.

This can help to establish the executive sponsor as a trusted advisor and point of contact and can also demonstrate the organisation's commitment to the success of the deal.

Activate Email Triggers When an Opportunity is Created, Nurtured or Qualified Out

Activating email triggers from a CRM platform can be beneficial for B2B marketing because it allows you to take certain actions based on specific events that occur. You can also get more information from your sales team and identify areas of improvement and how you can collaborate to ensure the opportunity progresses.

TOOLS FOR CONVERSION OPTIMISATION

Tools to Identify Website Visitors:

Leadfeeder

Factors.ai

The buyer's journey, clearer than ever | Clearbit Reveal

These tools help businesses identify and target potential leads from their website traffic.

With these tools you can easily track and identify potential leads, even if they don't fill out a form or make a purchase on your website. They provide detailed insights into the companies visiting your website and the pages they viewed. This information can be used to tailor your sales and marketing efforts and reach out to potential customers at the right time with the right message.

They also provide data on which elements of your site are most effective in driving conversions, such as sign-ups or demo bookings, based on factors like company size, revenue, location, and more. This information can be used to optimise your website and improve conversion rates.

Free Lead Enrichment & Scoring Tools

Zapier

MadKudu

Use Zapier and MadKudu to enrich and score leads for free. By using these tools, you can gain access to company information such as size, industry, and location, as well as other valuable data points. This can be especially useful for businesses looking to target specific types of leads or companies.

To take advantage of this tactic, you will need to have a Zapier premium plan or sign up for a free 7-day trial. By using lead enrichment and scoring tools, you can gain valuable insights into your leads and better target your marketing efforts, ultimately helping to increase conversions and grow your business.

WordPress Popup Plugin for More Email Subscribers - ConvertPlus

ConvertPlus is a powerful lead generation and conversion optimization tool that helps businesses increase the number of conversions on their website. By integrating with popular marketing platforms such as Google Analytics and MailChimp, ConvertPlus allows you to create targeted opt-in forms and pop-ups that capture leads and encourage conversions.

With ConvertPlus, you can easily create a range of opt-in forms and pop-ups, including lightbox pop-ups, slide-in forms, and floating bars. You can customise the appearance and content of your forms and pop-ups to match your brand and website and choose from a range of triggers to control when and how they are displayed to visitors. For example, you can set up a lightbox pop-up to appear when a visitor is about to leave your site, or a slide-in form to appear after a visitor has spent a certain amount of time on your page.

In addition to creating opt-in forms and pop-ups, ConvertPlus also offers a range of features to help you manage and nurture your leads. You can use the tool to segment your leads based on specific criteria, such as location or interests, and target your marketing efforts accordingly. You can also use ConvertPlus's built-in CRM to track and manage your interactions with leads, including emails, calls, and meetings.

Plezi One - Turn your website into a lead-generating machine

Plezi is a SaaS marketing automation software provider that has recently launched its new product, Plezi One, in public beta. This free and intuitive tool is designed to help small and medium-sized B2B companies transform their corporate websites into lead generation platforms.

Plezi One facilitates the generation of qualified leads by seamlessly adding forms with automated messages to companies' sites. It also allows users to understand what each lead is doing on the site and how their activity changes week after week, using clean dashboards. The main advantage of Plezi One is that it does not require any technical knowledge to use, making it a good choice for companies just starting their digital marketing efforts.

To use Plezi One, users can create forms that can be customised for different stages of the buying cycle. Forms are a convenient and direct way to turn anonymous visitors into qualified leads on a website and can be used to encourage visitors to get in touch, request quotes, or access various resources such as white papers, newsletters, and webinars. Plezi One also offers templates and smart fields to help users personalise follow-up emails that are automatically sent to people who have filled out the forms.

In addition to form creation, Plezi One also includes a Contacts tab where users can track and manage relationships with prospects

Axiom.ai

Axiom.ai is a digital marketing automation tool that utilises artificial intelligence to help businesses improve their customer experience, increase website traffic, generate leads, and enhance engagement with their customers. It allows you to set up automated workflows based on specific outcomes. Axiom.ai offers a free trial with up to 30 minutes of monthly run-time and a starter plan for $10/month that includes 5 hours of run time.

Jotform

Easily find and use 10,000 form templates that you can add to your website.

JotForm is a web-based platform that allows users to create and publish online forms, surveys, and polls. It offers a range of customizable templates and a drag-and-drop editor to make it easy for users to create professional-looking forms without any coding knowledge.

JotForm also provides a range of features to help users manage and analyse their collected data, including the ability to integrate with other tools such as Google Sheets and Salesforce, and to receive notifications when new responses are received.

JotForm is suitable for a wide range of use cases, including collecting customer feedback, registration forms, event sign-ups, and more. It offers various pricing plans to suit different needs, including a free plan with basic features and paid plans with additional functionality.

PART NINE:

ALIGNING SALES & MARKETING:

A MATCH MADE IN HEAVEN

INTRODUCTION

B2B sales statistics show the alignment of sales and marketing teams can lead to 38% higher sales win rates.[64]

MarketingProfs

In the current digital age, B2B buyers are active throughout the purchasing process and interact with both sales and marketing teams. Therefore, it is crucial for sales and marketing teams to collaborate closely to offer a consistent and tailored experience for the buyer.

Furthermore, as a company's sales and marketing teams grow, it can become increasingly challenging to ensure that they are working together effectively.

Proper alignment between these departments, sometimes referred to as *"S-Marketing"*, is crucial for targeting the right customers, generating conversions, and increasing sales.

The word S-Marketing is derived from the blend of the words sales and marketing and refers to a shared department at companies which dedicates to closing more business with a combined approach. Within it, there is a shared framework of goals and strategies backed by continual communication that enables these teams to work as a cohesive whole.

Look at these compelling Sales & Marketing Alignment Statistics:

- Well-aligned sales and marketing teams drive more than 200% revenue growth[65] from marketing tactics.
- Sales and marketing alignment can help your company become 67% better at closing deals [66].
- A Forrester research has found that highly aligned companies grow

---

[64] https://blog.hubspot.com/sales/stats-that-prove-the-power-of-smarketing
[65] https://www.invoca.com/blog/10-stats-that-will-drive-your-sales-marketing-alignment
[66] https://blog.marketo.com/2019/10/sales-marketing-alignment.html

19% faster and are 15% more profitable.[67]

---

[67] https://www.forrester.com/blogs/sales-executive-perspective-on-alignment/

TACTICS FOR SALES & MARKETING ALIGNMENT

If you are unsure of how to begin improving the alignment of your sales and marketing teams, consider implementing these proven tactics for integrating these departments.

Establish Common Goals

> **"Establishing pipeline and revenue contribution targets for marketing is critical; without agreement on goals, all alignment efforts are doomed to failure."[68]**
>
> Phil Harell
>
> VP Senior Research Director
>
> Forrester

The way sales and marketing teams measure success is often different which can lead to misalignment between the two teams.

Sales teams are typically focused on short-term impact metrics such as revenue and new clients, while marketing teams focus on leading indicators such as the number of leads.

This can result in a disconnect where the marketing team is producing a high volume of low-quality leads, which is not beneficial for the sales team.

To overcome this, it is important for sales and marketing teams to establish joint goals and equal levels of accountability. This can be achieved by setting pipeline and revenue contribution targets for both teams and tracking progress against these goals on an ongoing basis. The pipeline and revenue contribution expectations should be tailored to the customer segment, typically with higher expectations for small businesses and lower expectations for enterprise clients. By focusing on

---

[68] https://www.forrester.com/blogs/sales-executive-perspective-on-alignment/

joint goals, sales and marketing teams can improve alignment and achieve better results.

Communication and Transparency

Once the common goals have been established, effective communication and transparency are essential elements for achieving alignment between sales and marketing teams.

Clear and regular communication ensures that both teams are working towards these common goals, while transparency promotes trust and understanding, allowing teams to work more efficiently and effectively. Without these elements, collaboration and alignment can be difficult to achieve, leading to missed opportunities and lower results.

Organise Weekly or Bi-Weekly Pipeline Cadence Calls

A weekly pipeline cadence in B2B marketing refers to the process of regularly reviewing and updating the sales pipeline on a weekly basis. These calls or meetings involve all relevant departments and not just Sales and Marketing, but also Partnerships and the Sales Development Team.

The sales pipeline is a visual representation of the sales process and includes all the leads and opportunities that a company is currently working on.

A weekly pipeline cadence helps ensure that the sales team is on track to meet their goals and helps identify any bottlenecks or issues that may be impacting the sales process. It also allows for timely follow-up with leads and helps keep the sales process moving forward.

During a weekly pipeline review, the sales team may review the status of each lead and opportunity, identify any next steps that need to be taken, and update the sales forecast. The sales team may also review the performance of marketing campaigns and adjust their strategy as needed based on the results.

Attend Weekly Sales Meetings

If you are not organising regular pipeline cadence calls, you can ensure alignment between marketing and sales teams by attending the regular weekly sales meetings. In these weekly meetings, marketers can stay informed about the progress of the sales team, identify the gaps in the pipeline and offer assistance as needed.

It is recommended that marketers:

- go through the leads that have been delivered, discuss their progress and discuss ideas for optimisation.
- share information about marketing campaigns, content, and offers for the coming week.
- talk about ideas and feedback from the sales team for future marketing efforts, such as offers and blog posts.

Organise Monthly Marketing & Sales Leadership Meetings

Hold regular monthly meetings for marketing and sales leaders to strengthen collaboration and address any issues that may be causing misalignment.

Review results and assess the service-level agreement (SLA) between the two departments. During these meetings, they should discuss key metrics such as:

- the number of leads generated
- the percentage of leads accepted and worked on
- the lead-to-customer conversion rate
- Review of Marketing qualified leads (MQLs)

Spend Time Together

It can be beneficial for sales and marketing team members to spend time together in informal settings, such as at industry meetups, in-office happy hours, or conferences.

These types of events offer a chance for team members to get to know each other outside of the office and can help to foster better relationships and communication.

Internal Marketing Newsletters

Whether weekly or monthly, Internal marketing newsletters are important in B2B marketing for several reasons: They help keep employees informed, improve employee engagement, foster a sense of community, improve brand awareness, and facilitate cross-functional collaboration

To further improve sales and marketing alignment, these newsletters should feature highlights of the sales team's wins, new clients, and special accomplishments. It is also a good idea to include the profiles of individual salespeople. This not only helps to build morale and recognize the efforts of the sales team but also aligns marketing efforts with the sales team's goals. Additionally, highlighting the sales team members in the newsletter can also help build relationships between sales and marketing, as it allows everyone to better understand the people behind the numbers and strategies.

Publish Customer Win Announcements

As a B2B marketer, one effective strategy is to create internal customer win announcements that highlight important wins and the strategies used to achieve them. These announcements can be sent to all employees or to specific sales teams within a region or globally.

Internal customer win announcements serve multiple purposes. Firstly, they provide inspiration to the sales team by showcasing the success of others in the company. This can help to motivate the sales team to adopt similar strategies and approach potential clients with confidence.

Secondly, these announcements demonstrate to all employees the importance of the sales team's work and the impact it has on the company's overall performance. It can help to build morale and foster a sense of teamwork among all employees.

Finally, these announcements can also be used as a learning tool for the entire company. By sharing the strategies and tactics that led to success, other teams and departments can learn from the sales team's approach and potentially implement similar strategies in their own work.

In summary, creating internal customer win announcements is an effective way to inspire and motivate your sales team, demonstrate the importance of the sales team's work to all employees, and provide a learning opportunity for the entire company.

Support Lead Generation or Pipeline Build Ideas from Sales

One way to promote alignment is by having marketing support lead generation ideas from sales.

When a salesperson comes up with a lead generation idea, they are likely to have a deep understanding of the needs and pain points of the company's target audience. They may also have insights into how the company's products or services can be positioned to better meet those needs. By working with marketing to implement these ideas, the marketing team can create more effective campaigns and messages that will be more likely to convert leads into customers.

Additionally, the salesperson has a personal investment in the success of the idea and therefore is more likely to see it through and put in the necessary effort to make it successful. Owning the idea leads to a sense of ownership and accountability that are both critical to lead generation.

When both teams are working together and focused on the same goals, they can achieve greater success as a team.

Marketing should support lead generation ideas from sales as long as the idea makes sense.

TOOLS FOR SALES AND MARKETING ALIGNMENT

Gong

Gong, an AI-powered platform mainly used by sales teams, can also be utilised by marketers to gain valuable insights from sales calls. Its capabilities enable users to easily identify patterns and pinpoint key sections of the transcript, making it a valuable tool for conducting research and creating strategies.

Drift

Drift's platform is designed to increase revenue by converting more website visitors into valuable leads. It streamlines the process by providing a seamless transition from marketing to sales, using conversational marketing techniques to quickly turn leads into opportunities

Measure What Matters and Lead Strategic Growth | People.ai

People.ai provides marketers with unprecedented insight into their sales pipeline, allowing them to create more effective campaigns for nurturing, reactivating, and retaining customers

PART TEN:

KEEPING CUSTOMERS COMING BACK FOR MORE

INTRODUCTION

Only a 5% increase in customer retention can increase company revenue by 25-95%.[69]

HubSpot

Marketing efforts should also be geared on retention, upselling, building customer loyalty, and promoting advocacy. This will not only improve engagement and conversion rates, but also provide valuable insights for creating new campaigns.

A strong customer experience program should be based on the company's brand, values, and talent, and require close collaboration between Marketing and Customer Success teams. Additionally, businesses should prioritise customer retention because it is more cost-effective than acquiring new customers and helps build long-term, profitable relationships.

Research by Frederick Reichheld of Bain & Company along with Earl Sasser of the Harvard Business School have shown that improving customer retention by 5% can increase profits by 25-95%[70].

Automation can also help lower the expenses associated with customer retention.

Let's go through some ideas on how marketing can contribute to customer retention.

---

[69] https://blog.hubspot.com/service/customer-retention
[70] https://hbswk.hbs.edu/archive/the-economics-of-e-loyalty

TACTICS FOR CUSTOMER RETENTION

Nail the Customer Welcome

To retain customers, it is a good idea to send a welcome email or handwritten note to new customers, along with some branded promotional items (such as "SWAG" gifts) to form a welcome kit. Extra points if the note is from the founder. This letter should express the company's commitment to providing excellent service and exceeding customer expectations. This personalised touch will help build a better relationship with the customer, as few companies take the time to do this.

For software products, a personal message from the founder to users can also be displayed online after customers sign up for your product.

Basecamp does this well with a welcome note from Jason Fried, saying that users can contact him anytime in case of questions and give them his email and Twitter handle. This simple move adds a personal touch and makes users feel valued and welcomed.

Build a Community for Customers

Keep your customers up to date with all the latest tips and best practices of using your product by creating a community (Slack, Facebook/LinkedIn group or regular events or Customer Info Days, Regular Training and so on).

Users can get to know each other, exchange knowledge, and talk about how each of them uses your product. This results in levelling up your users' expertise in using your product, which makes them more likely to keep using it for longer.

Celebrate Milestones

Recognize and celebrate customer's accomplishments and milestones, such as when a project goes live or when a customer reaches an anniversary with your company.

This can be done through small gestures such as sending a gift or acknowledging the achievement on your company's social media. Making memories around your shared experiences helps to show the customer that their success is important to your business and helps to strengthen the relationship.

Run an Annual Customer Advisory Board

Involve select customers in the product strategy and direction by running a customer advisory board. This is a group of top customers who are invited to provide input and feedback on the direction of the product and the company.

By involving customers in this way, you show them that their opinions are valued and that their needs and preferences are being taken into consideration. This helps to foster a sense of ownership and loyalty among customers and can lead to improved retention.

Holding regular customer advisory board meetings allows for ongoing communication and collaboration with top customers, which can help to identify potential issues and areas for improvement. It is a win-win initiative because it also provides an opportunity to gather valuable customer insights and ideas that can help shape the direction of the product and the company.

Crowdsource Improvement Ideas

To invite more customers to be involved, you can encourage your users to let you know which improvements, features they'd like to have in your product, what new courses they'd like to see and so on.

Make it easy for them by placing a voting widget inside your product. It's a win-win situation: your users get features they need and feel heard, and you get quality feedback on what to build next.

Run Regular Customer Satisfaction Surveys

There are several strategies that businesses can use to improve customer retention in the B2B market with customer satisfaction surveys. Marketing can collaborate with Customer Success to regularly conduct surveys:

By conducting surveys on a regular basis, businesses can stay informed about their customers' needs and preferences and identify areas for improvement.

1. Ask for feedback: Asking customers for specific feedback on their experience with the company and its products or services can provide valuable insights for improving retention.
2. Act on feedback: It is important to not just gather feedback, but to also act on it. Showing customers that their feedback is being taken seriously and that changes are being made based on their input can increase satisfaction and loyalty.
3. Personalise communication: Using the information gathered from customer satisfaction surveys, businesses can personalise their communication and tailor their marketing efforts to meet the specific needs and preferences of their customers.
4. Offer incentives: Providing incentives for customers to complete satisfaction surveys can increase response rates and provide more accurate and comprehensive feedback.

Run Account-Based Engagement Emails

To retain customers, it is important to maintain their interest in your products, services, and brand.

For software companies, you can use data on how often customers use your platforms to create targeted engagement campaigns. For other types of businesses, it is important to create strategic email campaigns that provide value to customers and enhance their experience with your brand.

Publish Newsletters with Exclusive Content

Creating a newsletter with exclusive content for existing customers can be an effective way to improve engagement and strengthen relationships. One strategy is to segment newsletter subscribers and provide content that is tailored to their specific interests. This could include a newsletter from the company CEO with regular updates or education and training content that addresses the needs of the customer. Additionally, including interesting and engaging content that helps to build credibility for the company's brand can also increase engagement with the newsletter.

Use Reciprocity

To boost customer loyalty, reciprocity can be employed as a strategy. This social construct is known to increase loyalty by making the recipient feel an obligation to repay acts of kindness.

Two types of reciprocity [71] can be utilised in customer service according to HubSpot:

- **surprise**, like unexpectedly sending tickets for an event, and
- **trumpeted,** where the act of kindness is made obvious to the customer and goes beyond the typical scope of the relationship. Examples include taking behind-the-scenes photos and presenting them as a gift to the customer.

Run Reactivation Emails

Send an email after a period of inactivity encouraging users to go back to your product. You can incentivize them e.g., by giving them credits to use your product - they just need to return to the app to claim them.

Use Sign In Page for Product Updates

Use the otherwise unused space of your sign-in page to notify your users about new product updates. This will help faster feature adoption, which will make users get more value from your product, which in turn will improve their retention.

---

[71] https://blog.hubspot.com/service/customer-retention

TOOLS FOR CUSTOMER RETENTION

Reachdesk

Reachdesk is a solution that provides a streamlined way to manage corporate gifting campaigns. The platform allows you to easily source, send, track, and measure gifts, and includes features that allow you to evaluate the performance and ROI of your campaigns. With Reachdesk, you can improve customer retention by using personalised swag to onboard new customers and by providing rewards to existing customers for their engagement. With a G2 rating of 4.5, Reachdesk is an effective solution for businesses looking to improve their retention rate and make the most of their gifting budget.

Nolt

Nolt is a platform designed to manage customer requests and feedback in a clear and organised way, replacing the need for old spreadsheets. It allows customers to voice their ideas and feedback which can be used to improve the workplace. It costs $25 per month per board. The team is open to new ideas that can enhance the platform. Additionally, it includes a feature for creating and tracking a roadmap.

CustomerGauge

CustomerGauge is a B2B customer feedback software that has been ranked as the top choice by Gartner. Its unique approach, Account Experience, offers a comprehensive plan to enhance customer loyalty, decrease customer turnover, and increase customer referrals with a Net Promoter Score program. This solution is mainly aimed at medium and large B2B companies.

GrowSurf

Referral program software like GrowSurf automates the process of referral marketing and incentivized word-of-mouth to help businesses acquire new customers. This type of software also helps to increase loyalty and retention among existing customers.

Studies indicate that offering loyalty points and discounts can retain 53% of customers, while referral marketing accounts for 26% of customer retention.

Specifically, GrowSurf is a referral program software that offers B2B SaaS companies the ability to retain and attract customers by giving both referring and new users rewards such as gift cards, discounts, account credit, and even cash payouts. It seamlessly integrates with the sign-up process to track referrals and also automates reward fulfilment for a more convenient approach.

CLOSING REMARKS

Dear Reader,

I hope that you have found "The Ultimate B2B Marketing List: 200 Tactics You Need to Try" to be a valuable resource and that my passion for this field has come through in the pages of this book.

The tactics are designed to help you succeed, but it's important to focus on those that align with your marketing priorities. Don't just read this book and forget about it - take action to put the relevant tactics into practice.

While I have included a wide range of tactics in this book, there are many more out there that I haven't mentioned. If you're interested in learning those that didn't make the cut, you can visit my website and register your email to receive the list for free (exclusive for buyers of this book).

I plan to update this book annually to keep up with the fast-changing trends in B2B Marketing. You'll be able to receive updated versions in eBook format at a minimal cost. (Contact: me@jessica.schwarze.com).

Thank you for reading this book. I believe that you deserve to shine and be successful, and if this resource can contribute to that in any way, it would be an honour and a privilege for me as the author.

Sincerely,

Jessica

GLOSSARY

ABM (Account-Based Marketing): A strategy that focuses on identifying and targeting specific, high-value accounts with personalised campaigns.

A/B Testing: The process of comparing two versions of a website or marketing campaign to determine which performs better.

Analytics: The process of collecting and analysing data to understand and improve performance.

Brand Advocacy: The process of encouraging customers to promote a company's brand through word of mouth or social media.

Brand Awareness: The degree to which a target audience is familiar with and recognizes a company's brand.

Brand Identity: The visual and messaging elements that make up a company's brand, including its logo, colour scheme, and overall aesthetic.

Content Creation: The process of developing and producing various types of content, such as blog posts, infographics, videos, and social media posts, to support a company's marketing efforts.

Content Marketing: The process of creating and distributing valuable, relevant, and consistent content to attract and engage a clearly defined audience with the goal of driving profitable customer action.

CRM (Customer Relationship Management): The process of managing interactions with current and potential customers.

Customer Journey Map: A visual representation of the steps a customer goes through before, during, and after purchasing a product or service.

Customer Retention: The process of keeping current customers engaged and satisfied with a company's products or services.

Conversion: The process of turning a website visitor into a customer or lead.

Demand Generation: The process of creating and nurturing demand for a company's products or services through various marketing activities.

Email Marketing: The process of using email to promote products or services and build relationships with customers.

Event Marketing: The process of promoting a company or product through live events, such as trade shows or networking events.

Funnel: A visual representation of the journey a potential customer goes through before becoming a paying customer.

Gated Content: Content, such as white papers or e-books, that is only accessible to users who provide their contact information in exchange.

GIF: GIF stands for Graphics Interchange Format. A GIF is a short, animated image that can be used in digital marketing. They can be used to help make an advertisement, social media post, email, or blog more engaging and convey emotions in a more visual way.

GIPHY: GIPHY is a platform that allows users to search for, create, and share short, animated images known as GIFs (Graphics Interchange Format). GIPHY's database includes millions of GIFs that can be used for a variety of purposes, including in B2B marketing.

Growth hacking: A set of experiment-driven techniques to grow a business quickly and efficiently.

Inbound Marketing: The process of attracting, engaging, and delighting customers through relevant and helpful content and experiences.

Influencer Marketing: The process of partnering with industry experts or social media personalities to promote a brand or product.

KPI (Key Performance Indicator): A metric used to measure the success of a marketing or sales campaign.

Landing Page: A standalone web page designed to convert visitors into leads or customers, often used in conjunction with PPC or email marketing campaigns.

Lead: A potential customer who has shown interest in a company's products or services.

Lead Generation: The process of finding and cultivating potential customers.

Lead Qualification: The process of determining the potential value and fit of a lead for a company's products or services.

Lead Scoring: The process of assigning a numerical value to leads based on their level of engagement and likelihood of converting into a paying customer.

Long-Tail Keywords: Long-tail keywords are specific and longer phrases that web users type into search engines to find exactly what they're looking for. These keywords are typically more targeted and less competitive than short-tail keywords.

Marketing Automation: The use of software and technology to automate repetitive marketing tasks and improve efficiency.

Marketing Mix: The combination of elements that a company uses to promote its products or services, including product, price, place, promotion, people, process, and physical evidence.

Marketing Operations: The process of managing and coordinating all aspects of a company's marketing efforts, including strategy, budget, and technology.

Marketing Tools: The software and technology platforms used to support and automate marketing efforts, such as email marketing, marketing automation, analytics, and CRM. Examples include: Hubspot, Marketo, Pardot, MailChimp, Hootsuite, Google Analytics and others.

Outbound Marketing: The process of actively reaching out to potential customers through advertising, sales calls, email, and other forms of promotion.

Partner Marketing: The process of working with third-party partners to promote a company's products or services.

Persona: A fictional representation of a company's ideal customer, used to guide marketing and sales efforts.

PPC (Pay-Per-Click) Advertising: A form of online advertising in which the advertiser pays each time a user clicks on one of their ads.

PR (Public Relations): The process of managing a company's reputation and relationships with the media and the public.

Product Marketing: The process of positioning and promoting a company's products to its target audience.

Remarketing: The process of reaching out to customers who have previously shown interest in a company's products or services but did not convert.

Retargeting: The process of showing targeted ads to users who have previously interacted with a company's website or products.

ROAS (Return on Ad Spend): A metric used to measure the profitability of a company's advertising efforts, calculated by dividing revenue by ad spend.

ROI (Return on Investment): The measure of the profitability of an investment.

SEO (Search Engine Optimization): The process of optimising a website to rank higher in search engine results pages.

SEM (Search Engine Marketing): The process of using paid advertising on search engines to increase visibility and drive traffic to a website.

Sales & Marketing Alignment: The process of aligning the goals and strategies of the sales and marketing departments to ensure a seamless customer experience and maximum efficiency.

Short-Tail Keywords: Short-tail keywords are short and broad phrases that web users type into search engines. They are characterised by having one or two words, they are general, common, and highly competitive.

Social Media Marketing: The process of using social media platforms to promote products or services and build relationships with customers.

Targeting: The process of identifying and reaching a specific group of consumers or businesses that are most likely to be interested in a company's products or services. This can be done through demographic, geographic, or psychographic segmentation.

Website Optimization: The process of making changes to a website to improve its performance in terms of user experience, search engine rankings, conversion rates, and overall effectiveness in achieving business goals.

Printed in Poland
by Amazon Fulfillment
Poland Sp. z o.o., Wrocław
17 October 2023

9cc3892e-b9e3-4195-a62c-2c4bce1d127cR01